No Faith
in Religion

First published by O Books, 2009
O Books is an imprint of John Hunt Publishing Ltd., The Bothy, Deershot Lodge, Park Lane, Ropley,
Hants, SO24 0BE, UK
office1@o-books.net
www.o-books.net

Distribution in:	South Africa
	Alternative Books
UK and Europe	altbook@peterhyde.co.za
Orca Book Services	Tel: 021 555 4027 Fax: 021 447 1430
orders@orcabookservices.co.uk	
Tel: 01202 665432 Fax: 01202 666219	Text copyright John Saxbee 2008
Int. code (44)	
	Design: Stuart Davies
USA and Canada	
NBN	ISBN: 978 1 84694 220 4
custserv@nbnbooks.com	
Tel: 1 800 462 6420 Fax: 1 800 338 4550	All rights reserved. Except for brief quotations
	in critical articles or reviews, no part of this
Australia and New Zealand	book may be reproduced in any manner without
Brumby Books	prior written permission from the publishers.
sales@brumbybooks.com.au	
Tel: 61 3 9761 5535 Fax: 61 3 9761 7095	The rights of John Saxbee as author have been
	asserted in accordance with the Copyright,
Far East (offices in Singapore, Thailand,	Designs and Patents Act 1988.
Hong Kong, Taiwan)	
Pansing Distribution Pte Ltd	
kemal@pansing.com	A CIP catalogue record for this book is available
Tel: 65 6319 9939 Fax: 65 6462 5761	from the British Library.

Printed by Digital Book Print

O Books opera... a ... eth... ...lishing philos...phy in
all areas of its busi..., from its g...a...... ...; to
production and worldwide distribution.
This book is produced on FSC certified stock, within ISO14001
standards. The printer plants sufficient trees each year through
the Woodland Trust to absorb the level of emitted carbon in
its production.

No Faith
in Religion

Rt Revd Dr John Saxbee

BOOKS

Winchester, UK
Washington, USA

CONTENTS

Introduction   1

Chapter 1 Religionless Christianity and the Leap of Faith   15

Chapter 2 Faith, Religion and Redemption   28

Chapter 3 No End of Faith   39

Chapter 4 No Faith in the Church?   49

Chapter 5 Relics of Religion – Footprints of Faith   64

Chapter 6 Faith, Religion and Revelation   74

Chapter 7 Vicarious Faith or Religion-Lite?   85

Chapter 8 Ministers of Religion: People of Faith   96

Chapter 9 Crisis? What Crisis?   114

Chapter 10 Back to Modernity   129

Chapter 11 Evangelism Re-Visited   138

Conclusion   148

Introduction

In an opinion poll published in the Sunday Times on 2nd September 2007, 48% of those questioned thought that religion does more harm than good.

"Christianity was never meant to be complicated. It was never meant to be burdensome." (G. R. Evans).

"Martin gave up protesting his lack of religion to the grocer because the man was dying, after all, and for all Martin knew faith was the only thing that was keeping him going". (Kate Atkinson: *One Good Turn*. Black Swan 2006 p. 122).

If religion is characterised by the recruitment of God to serve our agendas, and faith is about putting our agendas at the service of God, then clearly there is too much religion in the world, and not enough faith.

All too often those having to respond to attacks on religion attempt to prove that its perceived evils are in fact the result of hijacking by political, socio-economic or psychological agendas which have little or nothing to do with religion itself. From the partition of India through the troubles in Northern Ireland to civil war in Iraq religion is identified as the key contributor to violence and social unrest. Rid the world of religion it is suggested, and the world will be rid of a major obstacle to peaceful co-existence and human flourishing. In his magisterial survey of European history since the French Revolution, Michael Burleigh focuses on the politics of religion and the religion of politics. He quotes Mussolini: "Facism is not only a party, it is a regime, it is not only a regime, but a faith, it is not only a faith, but a religion" (Michael Burleigh: *Sacred Causes*. Harper 2006 p. 57. See also *Earthly Powers*. Harper 2005).

Meanwhile, with an eye on the challenges facing the world in the 21st Century the eminent futurologist, James Martin, cites "the perversion of religions with philosophies that promote suicide killers" as a major threat, and reflects that "it would be an irony grander than any in great theatre if the religions that evolved from the teachings of the world's saintly prophets somehow prompted wars that wiped out civilization". (*The Meaning of the 21st Century* (Transworld Publishers 2007) p. 285 and 337). This theme is taken up with a vengeance by Christopher Hitchens in *God Is Not Great: The Case Against Religion* (Atlantic Books 2007), and if the 19th Century philosopher Baron von Clansewitz thought that "war is the extension of politics by other means" then Hitchens is not alone in saying: for politics read religion.

In response the claim is made that this is unfair and religious people cry foul. They maintain that religion is being made the scapegoat for human aggression, greed and tribal loyalties. Flawed humanity is seeking to project on to religion responsibility for evils motivated not by religious belief but by human degeneracy. The Spanish Inquisition has typically been singled out as the prime example of how religion pollutes and corrupts the fabric of society. Yet Toby Green, in his recent history of the Inquisition, is clear that its worst excesses were sanctioned by a secular drive to power rather than by religion (Toby Green: *Reign of Terror*. Macmillan 2007).

Still, the uncomfortable feeling remains that religion cannot be let off the hook quite so easily. After all, if religion can be so readily recruited to serve political or other causes, what is it about religion which makes it so vulnerable to hijack in this way? Indeed, might it be the case that in defining religion we have to build into our definition an acknowledgement that it is by its very nature at least a lightning conductor for other agendas, and possibly a core component in enabling those agendas to acquire adherents and gather momentum? If this is so, then those agendas are not so much parasitic upon religion as essential to its nature – and no amount of special pleading can rid religion of responsibility for what is done in its name.

Of course, what is done in the name of religion is often noble, altruistic and culturally enriching so that counterclaims can be registered against its critics. But it will not do for religious people to argue on the one hand that when evil is perpetrated in the name of religion then that is an example of religion being recruited for illicit purposes, whilst arguing on the other hand that good deeds carried out in the name of religion can be appropriately credited to religion itself. The worst is usually the corruption of the best, and it might be contended that good outcomes are to the credit of religion whilst evil perpetrated in the name of religion is necessarily evidence of it having been corrupted. Still the fact remains that for good or ill, God has been recruited to support what may or may not be God's agendas and it is this vulnerability to recruitment which partly defines religion over against faith.

Furthermore, there is little to be said for a grubby, self-serving calculus which seeks to show that, for all religion may be the cause of evils in the world these are outweighed by good things which can be attributed to religious beliefs and behaviour. Such a utilitarian calculus could see the scales tip in favour of religion as a force for good in the world, but at a price which those on the debit side should not be expected to pay. Dean Swift's question remains on the table: why is it that there is just enough religion in the world to make us hate one another, but not enough to make us love one another?

So let us accept that, so long as religion has this tendency to result in evil as well as good being done in its name, and there remains the strong possibility that religion is by its very nature conducive to being used and abused in this way, we must seriously question the role of religion in the world around us and look again at the relationship between faith and religion in the 21st Century.

This would presumably entail some kind of attempt at

precisely defining "religion" and "faith" in order to then evaluate them and map the relationship between them. However, in the case of religion, Wilfrid Cantwell Smith argued nearly 50 years ago in *The Meaning and End of Religion* (Macmillan 1962 p. 120) that the concept is inherently unstable, and should be dropped. Because it has come to mean so many things to so many people in a myriad of different eras and contexts it no longer conveys coherence or carries conviction. For example, Martyn Percy cites attempts by the likes of Feuerbach, Durkheim, Marx and Freud to explain religion in essentially reductionist terms but without attempting a strict definition (*Power and the Church*. Cassell 1998 pp. 2 – 6). Keith Ward sympathises with Smith but believes "it is difficult to see what possible alternative is being recommended" (*The Case for Religion* (Oneworld 2004) p. 12). He goes on to use the term as most appropriate for focusing "on the great debate between those who think that there are spiritual beings, realities other than those in space-time, to which humans can relate in feeling, knowledge and action, and those who deny it" (*op.cit.* p.18) – and thereby he basically offers his own definition. But it is hard to see how such a definition would differ significantly from a plausible definition of faith which, in its turn, has proved equally elusive when it comes to arriving at any kind of precise let alone agreed meaning. In Conversations on Religion (Continuum 2008) Mick Gordon and Chris Wilkinson invited a range of religious thinkers and commentators to define religion and faith respectively. The results are revealing but inconclusive, with an overall inclination to favour faith over religion but with little agreement or clarity as to the exact difference between them. Consequently, there remains a tendency to use these terms synonymously in a wide range of contexts and this might be felt to hole beneath the waterline any attempt to distinguish between them or weigh their respective characteristics.

Yet, whilst adherents tend to use religion and faith inter-changeably, it is noticeable that this is not typical of those who shun organised religion. "I am not religious", they say, "but ...". And then they proceed to articulate some kind of faith-based conviction which they believe to be real and valid, but which is not contained in what they mean by religion. (See Stephen Platten: *Rebuilding Jerusalem*. SPCK 2007 pages 143 and 158). They seem to know instinctively that to have faith is not the same as to subscribe to a religion, and there is an assumption in there somewhere that religion requires more formal commitments of them than they are ready or willing to undertake. There remains a sense that religion and faith are not the same and, most likely, of the two, religion will carry more negative, and faith more positive connotations. It is easy to dismiss this as an example of an immature spirituality predicated on cheap grace and a god who does not ask too much of us so long as we do not ask too much of him or her or it.

But this would be an unfair and unwise reaction. Many years ago W.E. Orchard declared the genius of the Church of England to be "that it had discovered just exactly how much religion the average Englishman (sic) can stand". Such comments are commonplace and might be summed up by the woman in a vox pop interview who liked the Church of England because "it leaves me alone". This can be taken to mean that mainstream Christianity in general, and the Church of England in particular, has reneged on religious rigour so as to settle for a mess of patronising pottage which might just keep the masses at least nominally affiliated. Yet looked at another way, it could be said that the kind of Anglicanism described here at its best has the good grace to foreswear the rules and regulations of religion so as to give some space for faith to be fanned into a flame without being stifled by the demands of dogmatism and over-zealous border controls. In other words, an environment is being created whereby faith can be given space to breathe with some implied recognition that religion and its associated agendas can suffocate rather than liberate the human spirit in its quest for such

5

meaning and purpose to life as only God can give.

This pushes us towards a definition of faith which could at least serve as a working definition for what follows: Faith is a disposition of the mind and will to entrust oneself and one's interests to the reality, reliability and benevolence of another.

This definition does not limit the applicability of faith–talk to spheres usually associated with spirituality and religious observance, and that is important because faith is not unique to either religion in general or Christianity in particular. But within the Judaeo-Christian tradition it is essentially a theological concept rooted in God who is free and who gives freedom. To that extent, it is a radically liberal concept with true freedom not being simply a matter of independence but, more profoundly, it is a matter of "being present to an other, of being in relation to an other, of gaining oneself by giving oneself to an other" (Peter C. Hodgson: *Liberal Theology: A Radical Vision*. Fortress Press 2007 p. 23). This freedom to give oneself in trust to another is itself a gift from God who is perfect freedom. It opens the way for a definition of religion along the following lines: Religion is the formalising of faith (for a mixture of motives and by means of *inter alia* doctrines and disciplines; credal statements and codes of behaviour; corporate membership and rites of initiation; cultic practices and personnel; legally constituted structures of organisation and authority; sacred scriptures, sites and symbols etc., etc.).

The core of this definition is very simple. Once faith is formalised in some way and for whatever reason, the dynamics of religion kick in. Some examples of how this is typically effected are offered in the bracket. This is not a necessarily negative process. Our definition of faith begs all sorts of questions about who or what the "other" is and to whom or to which people are entrusting themselves. Is such trust warranted, and on what criteria can reality, reliability and benevolence be established? Is "a disposition of the mind or will" sufficient to justify trust – and shouldn't faith be founded upon something firmer than mere "disposition"? These are legitimate questions which rightly preoccupy philosophers and theologians. But we must beware lest faith die the death of a thousand questions and qualifications as the formalising functions of religion become ends in themselves, with the priority and primacy of faith thereby compromised. The fundamental point is that the freedom inherent in faith is not typically experienced as a characteristic of religion, and that might begin to explain why more faith and less religion would be welcome in the wider world as well as the local Church.

So what underlies the following variations on the theme of religion and faith is not so much a felt need to achieve terminological clarity or analytical precision, as a sense that there are subtle and suggestive textures to these terms which seem to touch on a wide range of topics, from New Testament texts, through matters of doctrine and theological reflection, and on into contemporary challenges facing Church and Society. So let us turn our attention to these "subtle and suggestive textures" and tease out a little further what they might entail.

Skydiving is not my pastime of choice, but for the sake of a good cause most things are worth a try. So it was that I turned up at a local airfield to be briefed on the dos and don'ts of jumping out of an airplane at 15,000 feet. An Instructor spent 30 minutes introducing me to the kit and pressing home the importance of techniques essential to a safe free-fall stage, a well-timed pull of the parachute cord and a happy landing. This all got the attention and concentration it deserved so that I boarded the plane with rather more assurance than I had anticipated. However, when the moment came to fall forwards out of the plane, it all changed. Not one word of the Instructor's briefing could I remember. It was now a matter of hoping and praying that my instincts would be equal to the challenge and see me safely down to the landing site now scarcely visible so far beneath me. The free-fall was a blur, but the sheer will to survive ensured that the parachute opened on cue and the landing was messy but mercifully benign.

On reflection, I am clear that what got me up there was my faith in the instructions I had been given – and what got me down again was my faith in those everlasting arms which enfold us at all times but especially when we have forfeited all sense of being in control of our current situation let alone our eternal destiny.

In an analysis which fails to do full justice to the nuances and subtleties of biblical etymology, but which is still helpful for our purposes, Michael Frost and Alan Hirsch identify these two kinds of faith as "intellectual" and "existential" respectively (M. Frost and A. Hirsch *The Shape of Things to Come*. Hendrickson 2003 p. 133). Faith which is a kind of knowledge majoring on the intellectual content of belief is what is essentially conveyed by the Greek word for faith: *pistis*. This is the facet of faith which, when dominant, metamorphoses into religion. On the other hand, the Hebrew word *emunah* is less about intellectual assent and more about active trust which kicks in when our capacity to implement instructions and master techniques has been overwhelmed by the mind-numbing situation in which we find ourselves. On such an analysis, it was faith as *pistis* which gave me confidence to board that plane and position myself at the open door ready to jump. My assent to the instructions I had received, and my belief that the techniques were within my capabilities, made it possible for me to venture into a new and uncertain experience. But that only got me so far. It took more than head-knowledge and technical competence to get me to let go of the plane and launch into the unknown. I needed no end of *emunah* to see me safely to the ground as I put my trust in what my mind could not comprehend but my heart and soul had learned to rely on implicitly.

Both these facets of faith are essential to our understanding of what it means to be faithful. But Frost and Hirsch are right in their contention that "the trajectory of Western Christianity ... has been dominated by the Hellenistic concept over the Hebraic" (loc.cit.). The premium placed on dogmatism and doctrinal orthodoxy has seduced us into a false sense of intellectual security about what qualifies as faith and how we might come to possess it. This leads to a consequential insistence on knowing for sure where Truth in matters of faith is to be found, and who are the gatekeepers guarding the treasure of Truth against error. That in its turn leads to demands for the exclusion or even eradication of those unable or unwilling to signal their assent because they see God differently and want others to share their vision. A New York taxi-driver, possessed of an opinion on philosophy as on everything else, said of Descartes: "too much *cogito*, not enough *sum*". Well, Christendom may be said to be skewed by too much *pistis* and not enough *emunah*. It stands for factory-farm religion rather than free-range faith. It is this imbalance which makes religion vulnerable to those who need to vest their political and socio-economic ideologies with a semblance of theological authority. If they can insinuate their own credo into the doctrinal formulations of mainstream religion, or at least hitch a ride on them, then they have recruited God to serve their agendas, and the fault-lines in religion as *pistis*-focused are clearly exposed. It is also such an imbalance which drives religion into a defensive mode whereby it is more concerned with repelling boarders than attracting recruits.

Whilst *pistis* must have its place in the economy of faith, it is *emunah* which ensures that it is we who put ourselves at the service of God's purposes rather than God being hijacked to serve purposes not His own.

It is important to be clear that it is not a matter of *emunah* but not *pistis*. Those who follow H. Richard Niebuhr in caricaturing liberal theology as "A God without wrath brought men (sic) without sin into a kingdom without judgement through the ministrations of a Christ without a cross", tend to assume that there is no *pistis* element to liberal faith. It is deemed to be without credal content, with doctrine and dogma sacrificed on the altar of "keeping an open mind". But Lesslie Newbiggin famously quipped that it is all very well having an open mind, but not at both ends! Liberal Christianity remains anxious about that kind of closed-mindedness which not only believes that God's truth can be contained in theological definitions, but further believes that all such definitions necessary for salvation are now safely secured in one particular ecclesiastical locker. However, entertaining a healthy suspicion as to whether God's truth can ever be conclusively codified in such a way is not incompatible with a genuine conviction that God is real, God is good and God is both giver of life and stronger than death. Neither is it incompatible with a genuine conviction that evil is real, humanity is sinful and both can be redeemed by God's grace made manifest in Jesus Christ and mediated through the power of the Holy Spirit. Indeed, the greatest compliment paid by liberals to the importance of *pistis* in the economy of faith is contained in the number of alternative temporary and contemporary "creeds" which feature in liberal manifestos from time to time.

So *pistis* is important, but without *emunah* it has the tendency to fossilise faith and formalise it in such a way as to give us confidence when it comes to getting us to the edge of meaning, but lacks the active trust needed to make a leap of faith. G. R. Evans agrees: "Belief in the sense of holding a set of attitudes or opinions is not the same thing as belief in the sense of having faith." (*Belief: A Short History for Today*. Tauris 2006 p. viii). She then uses a quotation from Dostoevsky to underline that these distinctions "transform not only the way things look but the experience of life and the way it is lived":

"There must have been something stronger than the stake, the fire, even the habit of twenty years! There must have been an idea more powerful than any disaster, famine, torture, plague, leprosy and all that hell which mankind could not have borne without that one binding idea which directed men's minds and fertilized the springs of life". (*The Idiot*, III, iv Oxford World Classics 1992 p. 399).

Søren Kierkegaard traced several "Stages on Life's Way". From the aesthetic stage we pass through the ethical stage and on to the religious stage. Key choices have to be made by each individual on the way, and Jesus is offered as the perfect example to set before us as we make life's journey. Even when we reach the religious stage, a further choice needs to be made. We must choose between Religiousness A and Religiousness B. The former involves an act of will to leave behind all temporal aspirations in order to make room for what is eternal – to risk oneself upon "the seventy thousand fathoms of water". It is a daring act, like boarding a plane with a view to jumping out of it, but it remains an intellectual matter founded upon assent to propositions which are intermediate between us and God rather than being characterised by the immediacy of existential choice required by Religiousness B. This kind of religiousness "requires the abandonment of the supremacy of reason as well as of the security found in the objective – it necessarily involves, therefore, the enormous risk of staking one's life on something which may be mistaken". (Peter Vardy: *Kierkegaard*. Fount 1996 p 59).

What Kierkegaard calls Religiousness A and Religiousness B comes close to what is being distinguished here between religion and faith. Religiousness A is *pistis* without *emunah* whilst Religiousness B converts *pistis* into something infinitely more risky, uncertain and unpredictable but something ultimately more thrilling, fulfilling and redemptive. On our journey into God, religion can only at best be penultimate – it is faith which takes us over the abyss of apparent meaninglessness into the embrace of the everlasting arms.

So it is with Kierkegaard and his 20th Century echo, Dietrich Bonhoeffer, that we begin this excursion into the realms of religion and faith. They both challenged the way in which religion had hijacked Christianity and left it vulnerable to itself being hijacked by other causes eager to capitalise on its craven and accommodating disposition. Likewise, they both found their final uncompromising critiques of mainstream Christianity posthumously neutralised by those with vested interests in underwriting religion and over ruling faith. How different things might have been if Kierkegaard and Bonhoeffer had been taken seriously – and how very different things might have been if Nietzsche had read Kierkegaard! Perhaps the western world would have rightly relegated religion whilst strengthening its grip on faith to the benefit of those many millions whose lives have been blighted by the tyrannical excesses of quasi-religious ideologies and the vacuous banalities of post-modern relativism.

The next eight chapters apply this religion/faith dichotomy to some crucial areas of interest to those exploring what it might mean to be people of faith in a world saturated with religion. These are by way of being case studies with certain methodological implications which might be applicable in relation to other equally pressing concerns. The first is doctrinal, and argues that redemption is more of a faith commitment than a religious transaction. The second is biblical, and examines the endings of our four Gospels to show how the religious need for some kind of formal closure quickly qualified Mark's fearful yet faith-filled final verses. The third explores the "branding" of Christianity as a by-product of religion. From its earliest beginnings the Church has tended to formalise faith with buying into a particular religious brand becoming more important than the faith it purports to promote. What might a Church look like which clearly sees itself as fostering faith rather than advancing religion? The fourth focuses on relics as symbolic of a religious tendency to undermine God as the sole object of theology and faith by giving to words, actions and artefacts an objective status contrary to their true purpose. The fifth develops this theme in relation to Revelation which is currently a battleground not only between conservatives and liberals within Christianity, but within other Faiths as well. More faith and less religion will greatly assist in resolving crises which currently threaten not only Christian unity but peace and security on a global scale.

The remaining chapters address issues of crucial importance to the future of organised religion in general, and the role of the Church of England in particular. Is there still a place for "vicarious faith" when it comes to the relationship between Church and Society or is this simply a religious brand trying to hang on desperately to its market share? How mutually threatening are Ministers of Religion and People of Faith – indeed, are they mutually exclusive as representatives of religion and faith respectively? And does the promotion of lay ministry simply collude with "the cult of the amateur"? By no means least, a key question remains as to how this all affects the Gospel we proclaim. Recruiting foot soldiers to bolster the ranks of religion is one thing, and if our basic premise is correct then it is a thing as dangerous as it is undesirable. But attracting people into a faith which is infectious, life-enhancing and redemptive is something else again, with evangelism becoming essentially an invitation to take that leap of faith in imitation of Christ into the arms of the living God.

Finally, having begun with major figures on the European scene in the 19th and 20th Centuries we come right up to date with Richard Dawkins featuring prominently in a demonstration of how his attack on faith in God is in fact an attack on religion which can, perhaps ironically, enable him and others to embrace faith in all its fullness. Incidentally, the 19th Century also features prominently here in the shape of the Victorian "crisis of faith" which turns out to be just as much a "crisis of doubt". Is what has been described as "the re-enchantment of the West" evidence that a re-engagement with faith and spirituality could be about to happen again? Perhaps we are finding our way back to modernity and becoming appropriately secular in relation to religion, but significantly less secular when it comes to faith.

Whilst this represents an eclectic approach to the relationship between religion and faith, this approach may be appropriate because the issues penetrate the widest possible range of concerns in contemporary cultural and ecclesiastical contexts. From mediaeval polyphony to Andrew Lloyd Webber the development of a given theme through a sequence of variations has proved attractive to composers anxious to demonstrate the sometimes surprising potential of a simple melody. What follows is a modest attempt to do something similar with two concepts, religion and faith, which are usually seen as simply synonymous but which are in fact subtly different and subject to being interwoven in numerous complex and unexpected ways. There are many more variations on this theme than are attempted here, and I am conscious that in the interests of concision and a sharper focus I have tended to concentrate mainly on the Christian religion, rather than attempt a multi-faith approach. Likewise, where Church features in one or more of the variations it is the Church of England which tends to be cited by way of example and illustration. However, if the controlling theme has merit, and is worth pursuing, then others can devise further variations on a more expansive scale – and I hope they will.

Religionless Christianity and the Leap of Faith

"To represent a man who by preaching Christianity has attained and enjoyed in the greatest measure all possible worldly goods and enjoyment, to represent him as a witness to the truth is as ridiculous as to talk about a virgin who is surrounded by her numerous troop of children". (Søren Kierkegaard).

Søren Kierkegaard was a shadow boxer who turned out to be a bit of a bruiser. The shadow-boxing began when he first put pen to paper. From the first, he adopted a complicated scheme of indirect communication which resulted in a steady flow of astoundingly original and intensely challenging works appearing under a variety of pseudonyms. Whilst the baffled burghers of early 19th Century Copenhagen wondered about the true identity of Hilarius Bogbinder, Johannes Climacus and Nicholas Notabene, Kierkegaard wandered the streets as an eccentric man about town attracting respect and ridicule in almost equal measure. This method of indirect communication accorded with his pedagogic commitment to confront his readers with choices without the presumed authority of the author interposing itself between the text and the existential decisions to be made by the readers themselves. Significantly, *Either/Or* was one of his most celebrated works.

Midway through his writing career he underwent a profound religious experience which, together with a number of significant upheavals in is private life, prompted him to abandon pseudonymity and publish Christian Discourses in his own name. He had been brought up in a home where a rather dour brand of religiousness prevailed, and he regularly attended Lutheran Services, especially when J. P. Mynster, later Bishop of Sjaelland, was preaching. But his mid-life crisis caused

Kierkegaard to seriously challenge the legitimacy of the Established Church which consistently diluted the demands of discipleship. He abandoned plans to become a country parson and pursued a single-minded vocation "to introduce Christianity into Christendom". When Bishop Mynster died, and in the funeral eulogy was described as "a Witness to the Truth", the gloves came off and Kierkegaard's passionate but measured attempts to persuade Mynster to admit how his brand of Christianity fell short of Christ-like discipleship gave way to a sustained, populist and vitriolic attack on the Danish Lutheran Church in particular and the compromises of religion in general.

It all began in December 1854 with an article in a popular daily newspaper entitled: "Was Bishop Mynster a 'Witness to the Truth', one of the genuine witnesses to the truth – is this the truth?" After that the articles came thick and fast, and by the following May he was publishing his own broadsheet entitled "The Instant", which ran for 10 editions and where we read some of the most brilliant yet increasingly distasteful examples of Kierkegaard's polemical skill. He gradually moved on from attacking Mynster towards a more general assault on all representatives and manifestations of Christendom. Perhaps the most shameless of his attacks is contained in an article entitled *The Priests are Cannibals* in which he argues that the Priests feed themselves and their families off the flesh of the martyred saints. The shadow-boxer showed how he could sure pack a punch. The 10th edition of *The Instant* was ready for publication when Kierkegaard collapsed in the street and had to be taken to hospital where he died shortly afterwards on the 11th November 1855.

What became known as Kierkegaard's "Attack upon Christendom" stirred up a hornet's nest in Copenhagen, but as with the rest of Kierkegaard's authorship, it barely caused a ripple elsewhere. This reflected the fact that Danish was not a language widely read in Europe, and even in this period which became known as "the Golden Age" Copenhagen remained a relatively remote provincial city. Kierkegaard described himself as "a genius in a market town", and it was several decades before his work became familiar to German readers and well nigh a century before it found its way into English.

At the heart of Kierkegaard's attack upon Christendom was a parable which powerfully expresses the way in which religion succumbs to the State by diluting the requirements of Christianity so that the State can domesticate it to its own purposes and priorities:

"When a cabman sees a perfectly splendid horse, only 5 years old and without a blemish, the very ideal of what a horse should be, a fiery, snorting steed such as never was seen – then, says the cabman, 'No, that's a horse I can't bid on, nor can I afford to pay for it, and even if I could, it wouldn't be suitable for my use'. But when some half-score years have gone by, when that splendid horse is now spavined and lame, then the cabman says, 'Now I can bid on it, now I can pay for it and I can get so much use out of it or what's left of it, that I can really take pleasure in spending a little to feed it'.

So it is with the State and Christianity. With the proud air Christianity had when it first entered the world – 'No' – every state might say 'that religion I can't buy and not only that but I will say, Lord God deliver me from buying that religion, it would be certain to ruin me'. But then as Christianity in the course of some centuries became spavined, chest-foundered, bungled and generally made a mess of, then said the State, 'Yes, now I can bid for it, and with my cunning I perceive very well that I can have so much use and profit out of it that I can really take pleasure in spending a little to polish it up a bit'."

This is a classic example of how faith falls foul of religion which then, in its turn, finds itself prey to political and socio-economic interests intent upon colonising it to their own ends. Perhaps the established Church in 19th Century Denmark was not nearly so corrosive of the Christian faith as Kierkegaard contends, and he himself confessed to employing hyperbole in order to make his point. But he clearly saw the spectre of mass movements and destructive dictatorships just over the horizon, and the ways in which Communism and Fascism recruited the rhetoric and rituals of religion to attain and maintain power render his warnings all too prescient. He saw this coming long before Bertrand Russell in his *History of Western Philosophy* (1945) observed that Marx appealed to the masses because his terminology mimicked religious concepts: "Yahweh = Dialectical Materialism. The Messiah = Marx. The Elect = The Proletariat and Hell = Punishment of Capitalists". More recently, the Philosopher John Gray has argued that although religion is supposed to have been eradicated from western thought it in fact persists but now as a "black mass" of political and scientific myths (*Black Mass: Apocalyptic Religion and the Death of Utopia* London 2007). In her commentary on the evolution of Europe since the Second World War the travel writer Jan Morris comments that "even in my time un-Christian ideologies of Europe have … requisitioned the trappings of Christianity" (*Europe*. Faber & Faber 2006).

As we have seen, Kierkegaard promoted a path through life which must lead ultimately to an abyss of meaningless anxiety and despair or to a leap of faith. The seduction of religion with premiums placed on objective certainty and rationality must ultimately give way to an objective uncertainty where truth is subjectivity (not, please note, subjectivism), and the single individual stands alone before God. Reason has a vital role to play in discerning and interpreting the word and will of God, but then when we reach the very margins of meaning it is passionate inwardness rather than the objective externals of religion which will see us over the abyss. This is the essence of faith, and although religion will continue to play its part in the formulation and fashioning of corporate beliefs and practices, believers must not settle for such cheap grace as religion affords but must engage passionately with the demands of radial discipleship and trust in nothing but God's grace to see them home.

Of course, Kierkegaard had barely been laid to rest before critics set about blunting the full force of his devastating challenge to established Christianity. Their most effective weapon was the suggestion that Kierkegaard basically lost the plot towards the end of his life. He may have been a notable philosopher, psychologist, theologian and social commentator but sadly, they said, the Attack upon Christendom was nothing but the manic eruption of a mind gone wrong. No real evidence could be produced to support this patronising demolition of Kierkegaard's passionate protest, but the religious establishment found few voices raised against it and life in the "market town" soon settled down to business as usual.

Yet the truth is that the Attack was far from being an aberration. It was entirely consistent with Kierkegaard's authorship as a whole and was, to some extent, the almost inevitable outcome of all he had been trying to say to the comfortable Christianity of his fellow citizens who understood little and cared even less. That is usually the way it is when faith rails against religion – and dies in the attempt.

Dietrich Bonhoeffer was another who died in the attempt, and died at the hands of a tyrannical regime which classically recruited God and the trappings of religion to pursue its infernal purposes. Also, as with Kierkegaard, attempts have been made to blunt the radical thrust of Bonhoeffer's later writings from prison which seriously challenged the role of religion in a world come of age.

Bonhoeffer was initially attracted to Karl Barth who in his early work, influenced by Kierkegaard, offered a critique of religion. However, he soon became impatient with Barth's timidity when it came to standing up to the Nazis because, for Bonhoeffer, the Church is never merely the guardian of a revelation which has its origin and existence outside and beyond the cut and thrust of human life and relationships. Any religious talk of God as apart from the world rather than a part of the world is anathema to Bonhoeffer as his faith responds to the dramatic challenges facing German Christians in the wake of Hitler's rise to power and the imposition of Aryan laws on the Church and its leadership. In Bonhoeffer's view, it was not possible to detach discipleship from the cut and thrust of politics, and neither was it possible to cut the cost of discipleship by retreating into a form of personal piety which seeks to rise above, rather than work through, the difficult decisions demanded of us day by day.

Whilst for Kierkegaard it was the attempt to objectify faith and mediate it through systems of believing and belonging which fuelled his aversion to religion, and for Bonhoeffer it was the tendency to keep God and the Church apart from the world which drove him towards "religionless Christianity", the consequences in terms of cheap grace were the same. In *The Cost of Discipleship* Bonhoeffer wrote

"Cheap grace is the deadly enemy of our church. We are fighting today for costly grace.

Cheap grace means grace sold on the market like cheapjack's wares. The sacraments, the forgiveness of sin, and the consolations of religion are thrown away at cut prices. Grace is represented as the church's inexhaustible treasure, from which she showers blessings with generous hands, without asking questions or fixing limits. Grace without price; grace without cost! The essence of grace, we suppose, is that the account has been paid in advance; and because it has been paid, everything can be had for nothing. Since the cost was infinite, the possibilities of using and spending it are infinite."

This clearly mirrors much that we find in Kierkegaard's *Attack upon Christendom* with the implication that faith has been compromised by religion because religion dilutes the demands of discipleship either by reducing them to mere conditions of membership, or neutralising them so that they can be accommodated to the requirements of secular causes at a knock-down price and little effort. From the perspective of his prison cell, Bonhoeffer could only see Christianity becoming ever more compromised by its being in thrall to religion. Grace may be free, but it's not cheap, and it is Christendom which for Bonhoeffer as for Kierkegaard has led to the cheapening of grace and the enfeeblement of the Church. Kierkegaard sought to deal with the Grace issue by encouraging his contemporaries, and especially the religious leaders, to admit how far they fall short of God's demands and so lay claim to Grace as God's gift rather than their right. Bonhoeffer took a different line. The Enlightenment and the Age of Reason have enabled humankind to "come of age" in so far as it was no longer expected that God could solve all personal and social problems, or that human responsibility could be evaded. People were less inclined to call on God as a stop-gap to act as an explanation for things we cannot explain ourselves – a metaphysical being beyond the world who can be summoned into action when required. To that extent, argued Bonhoeffer, the modern world has cast off the garment of "religion" , by which he meant individualistic concern for one's own soul, or the God of the gaps who intervenes from beyond to influence what goes on in the world.

The "religious" view of God failed, says, Bonhoeffer, to take the Bible seriously. The Age of Science, of "man come of age" has helped us to see that it is only when godless people push God out of the world on to the cross that, in his weakness and power-lessness he is able to be with us and help us. To be a Christian does not mean being religious in a particular way – performing religious acts or working to cultivate a religious turn of mind – rather, it is about getting stuck in to secular life and thereby sharing in God's suffering in a godless world. "Christians stand by God in his hour of grieving" – this quotation from one of his letters from prison echoes the Garden of Gethsemane and reinforces Bonheoffer's view that the answer to the question "Who Stands Fast?" – posed in a Christmas message in 1942 – is that having stood by our neighbour, especially when that neighbour is a stranger to us (see *Sanctorum communio*); having stood by our principles, especially with respect to fulfilling our responsibilities as God's deputies in feeding the hungry, housing the homeless, establishing justice (see *Ethics*) and refusing to compromise with evil (see *Cost of Discipleship*); having stood fast against the enemy (see his speeches and writings connected with the Church struggle and the conspiracy against Hitler) and having stood up for humanity in all the concrete realities of joy and sorrow, we are above all to stand by God who suffers in the midst of the world. John Godsey sums it up like this:

"Bonhoeffer had no use for a false piety that ignores the world or a false worldliness that ignores God. His plea for a non religious, this-worldly faith is based solely on God's relation to the world in Christ. Such faith neither idolizes the world nor writes it off. The Christian life is one of proclamation and praise, of prayer and doing right; opening the mouth for those who cannot speak and risking acts of liberation on behalf of the oppressed. Only a life so lived avoids 'cheap grace' and witnesses to the love of God for the world". (*The Modern Theologians*. Edited David F. Ford. Blackwell 1989 Vol I p 65).It was that kind of life Bonhoeffer sought to live, and we can only speculate how his life and thought might have developed had he lived to fulfil the promise of those 39 years and to work out in detail the seminal ideas which have so influenced radical theologians in all the mainstream Churches.

Theo Hobson is clear that, in spite of attempts to rein in Bonhoeffer's radical tendencies by the likes of Stanley Hauerwas (*Performing the Faith: Bonhoeffer and the Practice of Nonviolence* (SPCK 2004), Clifford Green (*Cambridge Companion to Bonhoeffer*) and Stephen Plant (*Bonhoeffer* Continuum 2004), Bonhoeffer was set to launch a thoroughgoing attack on the Church so that "ecclesiastical authority is what he means by the sort of religion we must leave behind ... The grown-up world is the one that no longer needs the direction of the Church." (*Bonhoeffer's Ghost.* Theology Nov/Dec 2006 p 446). Hobson concludes:

"The desire of recent critics to rescue Bonhoeffer from the appearance of liberalism tells us more about the nervous conservatism that dominates theology than it does about Bonhoeffer himself. An honest appraisal of Bonhoeffer's development may help contemporary theology to rethink its attitude to 'liberalism'. Guided by Barthians on the one hand, and postmodern Catholics on the other, theology tends to believe that an interest in liberalism is tantamount to suicide. Bonhoeffer urges us to be less scared: he shows that theological liberalism is intimately related to the Pauline and Lutheran passion for freedom. If we are seriously to ask what 'freedom from the law' might mean today, we must be ready to follow Bonhoeffer, all the way."

To follow Bonhoeffer "all the way" is effectively to follow him along a path already marked out by Kierkegaard and which leads to faith rather than religion – *emunah* rather than *pistis* – as the ultimate expression of Christian discipleship. For both Kierkegaard and Bonhoeffer religion provided a base camp from which they ventured into the challenging uncertainties of existential faith where the choices which really matter are choices which cannot be made for us by others – especially when these others are religious personages with a vested interest in offering us grace on the cheap or discipleship at no cost. This is a robust faith which cost Kierkegaard and Bonhoeffer a great deal and which calls into question any attempts to criticise Christianity as but a crutch to support enfeebled and infantilised human beings who have taken refuge in otherworldly myths because they cannot stand too much reality.

Which prompts the question: what if Nietzsche had read Kierkegaard? This question is posed by Habib Malik (*Receiving*

Søren Kierkegaard: The Early Impact and Transmission of His Thought CUA Press 1954 p. 394) and it is an echo of Theodor Haeckers plaintive observation in 1913: "If only he (Nietzsche) had discovered Christian faith as Kierkegaard did, he could have been the source of a tremendous spiritual rebirth". (*Sören Kierkegaard und die Philosophie der Innerlichkeit*). Although one of Kierkegaard's earliest interpreters, Georg Brandes, explicitly made links between Kierkegaard and Nietzsche, and at the end of *Ecce Homo* Nietzsche showed himself aware of Brandes work, there is no evidence that he had direct acquaintance with Kierkegaard's writings. What difference might it have made if he had?

Well, for Hacker, Nietzsche's passion, inwardness, solitary suffering and "valiant and pure life" reminded him of Kierkegaard and had more to do with Christianity than meets the eye. In other words, Nietzsche might have found a good deal of fellow-feeling with Kierkegaard and then, perhaps, he would have also found Kierkegaard's Christianity to be a faith he, too, could expound and embrace. Whilst this is highly speculative it is not far fetched, and this impression is reinforced when we see how Kierkegaard and Nietzsche compare in their contempt for Christianity corrupted by Christendom. Nietzsche's view is well summarised by Curtis Cate:

"It was precisely because Christianity had ceased to be harsh and exacting ... and had instead grown smug, complacent, soft and flabby, that Nietzsche held it in such withering contempt. Like so much in the modern world, it had been riddled and eaten through and through by the wood-worm of democratic optimism and its categorical imperative: Christianity too must be tailored to popular wishes. Ground under in the process was the very notion of the sacred, of something to be revered precisely because it is not on our level but higher, nobler, and in the sublimest sense beyond Man's (sic) reach". (*Friedrich Nietzsche*. Hutchingson 2002 p xxi).

Like Kierkegaard, Nietzsche not only laments the way in which religion panders to the *bourgoisement* of belief but also depicts theologians, priests and church leaders as propagating "vicious frauds ... systems of cruelty on the strength of which the priest became and remained master" (*The Antichrist: An attempted Criticism of Christianity*. Aphorism 54). In *The Will to Power* (Aphorism 493) it is clear that for Nietzsche religion serves primarily to comfort vulnerable people who end up being manipulated and dehumanised in the process (see Anthony Thistleton: *Interpreting God and the Postmodern Self*. T.& T. Clark 1995). So Nietzsche shared many or even most of Kierkegaard's concerns about religion in general, and the Christianity of Christendom in particular. However, whereas Kierkegaard saw beyond religion (Religiousness A) to faith (Religiousness B), Nietzsche settles for the mere recurrence of experience over and over again and a New Man who affirms not God but himself and this ideal man, the superman, is the one who has sufficient will power to will this recurrence "insatiably calling '*da capo*', not only to himself but to the whole pageant of existence" (*Beyond Good and Evil*. Aphorism 56). Something like Kierkegaard's Religiousness A (*pistis*?) will still be needed to subdue and content the masses, but it is those with the Will to Power who will positively embrace Fate – and Fate rather than Faith (*emunah*?) ultimately commands the Olympian heights of human fulfilment.

All this is tosh, of course, and dangerous tosh because on the way to his Big Idea Nietzsche casts aside not only transcendent or metaphysical meaning, but also the very idea of meaning itself as all language is illusory, all truth claims are bids for power and all so-called facts are nothing but interpretations. Out of this melange of more or less incoherent aphorisms emerged post-modernism, with its pretentious cynicism, subjectivism and a "whatever" approach to Truth. All that in addition to the evils of 20th Century totalitarianism which fed all too readily on

Nietzsche's brand of materialistic humanism.

Yet Nietzsche saw so many things in the same way Kierkegaard saw them. He saw religion as a pale reflection of what it might have been so that it was all too attractive to those anxious to hitch God to their particular political or ideological bandwagon. Yet instead of attacking that kind of religion and transcending it with a faith far more noble and authentic, Nietzsche joins the bandwaggoners in recruiting religion to serve his own deluded fantasies. He saw the need for human values to be revisited in the light of a higher order of things, but whereas Kierkegaard postulated "a teleological suspension of the ethical" predicated on God's sovereign will Nietzsche proposes "a transvaluation of values" which is the ultimate capitulation to meaninglessness if it is on human capacities alone we must rely in our search for values which endure. He even echoes Kierkegaard in his emphasis on "the solitary individual" facing "existential choices" in that "Moment" when time and eternity intersect. Yet Nietzsche's lofty elevation and celebration of the individual and his or her moment of critical choice dissolves into what might be called an Oliver Twist moment: "Is *that* life? Very well! The same again!" If only Nietzsche had read Kierkegaard so that over and beyond the realms of religion which he rightly relegated to at best penultimate significance, he might have found a faith for humanity come of age in the image of Bonhoeffer's God rather than in the hubristic image of its own narcissistic self.

Kierkegaard, Nietzsche and Bonhoeffer have been critical to the evolution of western philosophy and theology over the past 150 years. Others have consolidated or contested their ideas, but they have done so as those who stand on the shoulders of giants. As pioneers venturing out from the base-camp of religion they each found their way to a place where return to base was inconceivable and only the embracing of Fate or a leap of faith into the arms of God remained as viable options. For each of them religion entailed the recruitment of God to serve human agendas. For Kierkegaard and Bonhoeffer, though sadly not for Nietzsche, faith as the placing of ourselves at the service of God's agendas came ever more sharply into focus. They stand sentinel for all those who continue to find no faith in religion.

Faith, Religion and Redemption

"The opposite of faith is not doubt, but sin". (Søren Kierkegaard)

We saw earlier that Kierkegaard could pack a punch, and this quote is one of his most powerful. Its power lies in the fact that across the widest possible spectrum of people, believers and non-believers alike, sin is seen as the core business of religion and few would link it to profession or denial of faith, notwithstanding the Epistle to the Romans: "For whatever does not proceed from faith is sin" (Chapter 14 vs. 23).

From the earliest days of Christianity there has emerged a complex and generally uncompromising apparatus for defining sin and dealing with it. Sin has not been seen as incompatible with faith. You may be acting inconsistently or even hypocritically when you sin, but you would still be numbered amongst the faithful. Indeed, the whole superstructure of confession, penance and absolution was designed to keep the faithful faithful, and only in the most extreme cases would anathema and expulsions be deemed appropriate. Corrupt manipulation of the apparatus of penance was a key factor in the build up of popular resentment on the eve of the Reformation, especially in relation to the selling and mis-selling of indulgences. But even the most zealous of the reformers never doubted that sin would remain the legitimate business of organised religion – and it is arguable that cultivating a consciousness of sin and the requirement to do public penance was at least as important to the leaders of Protestantism as it had been to their Catholic predecessors.

One of the no doubt unintended consequences of this institutionalisation of sin and forgiveness was that it tended to major on what Mark Biddle calls "the sin as crime" model (*Missing the Mark: Sin and its Consequences in Biblical Theology* Abingdon 2005). Biddle argues that

"In the West, the dominant model of sin and salvation – developed especially in the thought of Tertullian, Augustine, Anselm and Abelard – has long rested on a courtroom analogy. Human beings in wilful rebellion against God's authority violate God's law. Their crime incurs the penalty of death. God's perfect and absolute sense of justice requires the execution of the penalty. The only means whereby both the pure justice of God can be satisfied and the mercy of God can be made manifest involves God's willingness to assume the guilt and pay the penalty. In order to do so, God becomes incarnate and dies in humanity's stead. "

The 'sin as crime' metaphor, with its emphasis on the juridical, the individual, and wilful rebellion, and its interests in assignment of guilt and exaction of punishment, address certain aspects of the problem of human experience. Yet although dominant in the Western popular mind, it does not fully reflect the biblical witness, nor provide a sufficient basis for the Church's ministry in addressing human wrongdoing and its consequences ... In fact, although the 'sin as crime' metaphor dominates the Western popular mind, academic theologians, especially since the middle decades of the twentieth century, have increasingly recognised its shortcomings and offered a wide variety of critiques and alternative models" (p vii).

This extended quotation is followed by the first of many biblical passages analysed by Biddle to demonstrate the limitations of the "sin as crime" approach. So a further quotation is in order:

"The dominant Western model of sin does not equate fully with the biblical description of sin, the problem with being human. One well-known biblical example illustrates the point very clearly. King David committed adultery with Bathsheba, the wife of Uriah the Hittite and commissioned the murder of Uriah to conceal the crime (2 Sam.11). He must have been fully aware in both cases that his actions were wrong, contrary to the express will of Israel's God. He 'wilfully rebelled'. The juridical understanding well describes the nature of his sin. Nathan's message to David was on point: 'You are the sinner, you deserve the penalty' (2 Sam 12:7). Likewise, David's admission of guilt and successful plea for forgiveness were entirely appropriate (2 Sam 12:13). So far, as a biblical example of the dynamics of sin, the interaction between the king and the prophet corresponds to the Church's conventional treatment of sin: it is a wilful crime deserving of punishment, but a merciful God will commute the sentence for one who is truly repentant. The church's only role is to call the sinner to account and to offer the promise of forgiveness to the penitent."

"The biblical account goes on, however, to relate Nathan's triple prediction of disaster for David and his household (2 Sam 12: 10-14). Although forgiven, David's sin has its own vitality and will replicate in the lives of his children. David, as father and king, has created a system of interactions that will ultimately bring one of his daughters and three of his sons to ruin at the hands of other members of the king's family. The nation will experience civil war and long-term political unrest. The royal court will be torn by intrigue (2 Sam 13 – 1 Kings 2)".

Biddle then goes on to show how "the legal model for sin fails adequately to describe the full scope of a situation such as that created by David's sin with Bathsheba, and it also cannot provide a full range of tools for ministering to the full range of human pain and sorrow. The dynamics of sin in everyday life often more closely resemble the complexity of the aftermath of David's sin with Bathsheba than the simplicity of the 'sin as crime' model".

So the upshot of all this is that there is more to sin than meets the eye – at least the all too forensic eye of the heavenly courts determining guilt and dispensing justice. We can fully appreciate that this forensic approach appeals to the rules and regulations culture beloved of religious institutions and their functionaries. Those who have the scales of justice at their disposal are in possession of immense power over people's lives, and the outriders of religion in full cry after their sinful prey is never a pretty sight!

Furthermore, one of the reasons why religion is courted and colonised by ungodly causes is the access this gives to the apparatus of spiritual discipline and jurisprudence to further their ends. The idea of the Church of England as the Tory Party at prayer now sounds rather clichéd and passé, but the fact that it could ever have been considered plausible indicates that the Church as an ally in keeping the lower classes in order was an attractive option to those with a vested interest in preserving their own privileges. This is partly what Marx meant by describing religion as the opium of the people – by its threats of divine punishment and its promises of eternal rewards for good i.e. subservient behaviour the Church cheerfully colluded with socio-economic inequalities and injustices which had precious little to do with the Christian gospel. Further shameful examples can be cited in relation to slavery, apartheid, anti-semitism, inhumane penal systems and the subjugation of women. If your particular ideology can be backed by spiritual as well as secular sanctions then your position is significantly strengthened, and in certain societies will be rendered virtually impregnable.

This leads inexorably to the conclusion that sin and its consequences are too important to be left to religion which seems to be pathologically inclined towards prosecution and retribution rather than redemption and restoration. There is no doubt that this forensic approach to rebellion against God's word and will is evident in the Bible and Biddle is the first to acknowledge that this is so. Yet he is surely right to point out that the biblical approach to such rebelliousness reaches way beyond what the religio-legalistic approach can possibly convey. And if he is right about that, then Kierkegaard also needs to be taken seriously. Sin has more to do with faith than religion – and so does redemption.

As we have seen, faith is about putting ourselves at the service of God and God's agendas. It is about entrusting ourselves to God and, very often, to other people as the emissaries of God's love and grace. It kicks in when our own ability to know what is going on, be in control and take responsibility has deserted us. If we only rely on the "sin as crime" model we never move out of the sphere of self-control and personal responsibility. This model is predicated on establishing who was controlling the situation of wrongdoing and, therefore, who is ultimately responsible. It simply does not deal with situations where those affected by a sinful act, such as David's with Bathsheba, find themselves caught up in a cycle of evil deeds and painful consequences for which they have no ultimate responsibility and over which they have no significant control. Here the rhetoric and rigours of religion simply do not apply. Only faith can rescue us from the vicious cycle of sin and enrol us on the virtuous cycle of salvation. To quote Biddle again: "The effects of sin cannot be remedied merely by a transaction analogous to forgiving a debt … Significantly, the New Testament claims that the fundamental problem in human existence is lack of faith, a faulty sense of trust in God". (pp xviii and 12).

The opposite of faith is not doubt, but sin. If this is so, then faith as the antidote to sin is necessarily key to our understanding of redemption, and to this we now turn.

Those two giants of German culture, Nietzsche and Goethe had things to say about redemption. For Nietzsche ultimate redemption is to say to life "*da capo*" – let's live it all over again. For Goethe it was Faust's love of life – despite all his suffering and despite the suffering that he caused others – that redeems him (John Armstrong: *Love, Life, Goethe* Penguin 2006 p. 417).

Meanwhile, in Britain the romantic poets were extolling and celebrating "the redemptive power of nature" (see Adam Sisman: *The Friendship – Wordsworth and Coleridge* Harper Collins 2006). Coleridge's *Ancient Mariner* and Wordsworth's *Peter Bell* relied on an albatross and a donkey respectively to tell the stories of bad men eventually frightened into good.

How pathetic – in all the usual senses of the word. To say yes to living the same life over again may be courageous, but it is hardly redemptive. After all, by definition, it will involve doing nothing differently and what is redemption if it is not to do with making a difference? And what does Faust's stoical determination to love life actually do for those he has harmed along the way? His attitude is hardly redemptive, for what is redemption if it is not to do with somehow making a positive difference to those whose suffering we have caused? And what about the redemptive power of nature? Well there can be little doubt that Nature has a great deal to teach us about human nature, but still there is the whiff of idolatry around relying on the creature for a redemption which ultimately relies upon faith in the Creator alone. That the creature can be revelatory of our redemptive God there can be no doubt, but only so long as we acknowledge that the creature is just that – a creature.

However, what these examples illustrate is the way in which the language of redemption is equally at home in literary, philosophical, cultural, theological and numerous other contexts. But these contexts are not mutually exclusive so that what people mean when they use words like redeem and redemption is coloured by many kinds of usage. It is certain that the theological meaning of these words has been enriched by their interaction with usage in other contexts, but we do need to be on our guard lest confusion rather than clarity ensue.

In his intriguing book *Imagining Redemption* (Westminster Press 2005) to which I am particularly indebted for this section, David H. Kelsey carefully distinguishes between redemption relating to what people do, and redemption in relation to what people undergo. This links into our observations on the nature of sin as being, on the one hand, about the act of sin and the guilt of the sinner, and on the other hand, about how the after effects of sinful actions infect the lives and well-being of others who bear no responsibility for the original offence. We noted that a forensic approach based on one or more of the myriad theories of the atonement on offer in the Bible and in Christian teaching through the centuries might serve to save the sinner, expiate their sin and put them right with God. But what difference does that make to those who undergo the consequences of that sin even to the third and fourth generation? An understanding of God's redemptive love which only addresses the guilt of the offender, and God's right to exact retribution through the death of Jesus so that the sinner can be saved, is at best inadequate and at worst immoral. So we must extend our understanding of redemption so as to encompass within its generous economy not only sinful acts and their agents, but also evil consequences and those who experience them.

Yet we must go further still. For a great deal of the pain and suffering experienced in our world cannot be attributed directly, or even indirectly, to sinful acts perpetrated by whomsoever. Even if we were to accept some sort of doctrine of an original sin committed by humankind's original parents in a faraway garden during the early days of Creation – and how sadly prosaic and theologically uncouth such an acceptance would be – still that will do little to register on the radar of those searching for some kind of redemptive meaning in the midst of their human predicament. Perhaps we have to think rather less about original sinners and rather more about original victims. Kelsey uses as his controlling case-study the downward spiral of pain and bewilderment consequent upon the brain damage caused to a young boy following the flare-up of a rare viral condition leading to the total devastation of his family and, finally, the suicide of his mother. But we all know of countless other examples which could be cited, and which provoke the question: but where is redemption in all of this – is redemption possible?

On the face of it, although as Christians our first instinct in trying to answer such a question is to reach for our Bible, on this occasion that might not prove so helpful. After all, the term is drawn from the worlds of slavery, commercial transactions and the ransoming of prisoners from captivity. Gerald O'Collins sees this background as helping "to shape the cultural setting in which New Testament Christians proclaimed Christ as "redeeming", "buying", "ransoming", "freeing", or "liberating" "us", "you", "his people", "Israel", "many" or "all" (*The Oxford Companion to Christian Thought* p. 598). Apart from staking a claim for a place in the Guinness Books of Records as the sentence with the largest number of quotation marks, this does convey a sense of the richness but also the risks involved in describing Jesus as Redeemer. The associations with the slave-owning culture of the classical world remains all too dominant, and although nowhere does the New Testament speak of a price or ransom being literally or even metaphysically paid to someone (e.g. God or the Devil), in later Christian teaching we see "ransom" taken as if it described literally some kind of transaction. This put redemption on all fours with "sin as crime" in the sense that it falls well within the comfort zone of religion. If the power and control which goes with defining and dealing with sin sits easily with what we mean by religion, then so does an understanding of redemption which places within the control of religious institutions and their representatives the means whereby the ransom paid by Jesus can secure release and restoration.

So alongside the biblical language of redemption we can helpfully appeal to popular usage to inform our theological understanding and lead us to see that it is faith rather than religion which speaks most into human crises illustrated by that brain-damaged boy and the disintegration of his family through no apparent fault of his or theirs.

Kelsey majors on three familiar ways in which the language of redemption features in popular usage:

1. We speak of someone redeeming a poor performance or poor behaviour in the past by superior performance or behaviour in the present. So a criminal whose violence and drug dealing have damaged people is said to redeem himself if, on release from prison, he becomes a drug counsellor.

2. We speak of redemption in terms of regaining possession of something in exchange for a payment to e.g. a pawnbroker. That which was under another's control has now been restored to its rightful owner.

3. We speak of redemption when, for instance a manufacturer includes a voucher with a product that the buyer can "redeem" for cash or goods. The usage became particularly popular in the days of Green Shield Stamps!

It is not difficult to see how Christianity interacts with each of these popular usages. We do talk of God relating redemptively when God in some way "makes up for" bad experiences or behaviours, and their consequences, for which God may or may not be held responsible but which God will not allow to go unheeded or unaddressed. So Jesus' promises to be with us always, even to the end of time (Matthew 28 vs. 20), and to not leave us comfortless (John 14 vs. 18) carry redemptive significance because they hold out the prospect of God's presence through Christ, and in the power of the Holy Spirit, making a positive difference to the situations in which people find themselves. Where afflicted people have faith in God's presence – that underneath are the everlasting arms – then that which was bad is made better, and therein there is redemption.

Again, we do talk of God relating redemptively when God releases people and situations from ungodly i.e. alien and oppressive control. Even though this has all too often been seen exclusively in terms of God freeing people from evil forces and influences upon their lives, there is a way of understanding this more in terms of God's love than God's power. Or, rather, the emphasis is on the power of love than the love of power. The classical Problem of Evil can be expressed as God being either Power without Love (He could prevent suffering but chooses not to) or Love without Power (He dearly wants to prevent suffering but cannot). But there is a third way. God is Power in Love with the world. When we know ourselves to be loved by God, and we know that God has lived and suffered and died for that love, then the hostile powers of anger, guilt, self-pity and alienation which so bind us in situations of extreme suffering and sorrow are seen for what they are – ultimately transfigured by God who loves us as we are, loves us too much to leave us that way, and lifts us out of our thrall to death–dealing despair by the power of Christ's resurrection. Where afflicted people have such faith in God's love, then that which was bad is made better, and therein there is redemption.

Yet again, we do talk of God relating redemptively when God actually fulfils a promise He has made explicitly to humankind. The key promise of New Testament Christianity is that God in Christ is inaugurating a new creation:

"The Apostle Paul, writing as our earliest witness to Jesus' resurrection appearances, sees the resurrection as the event in which God begins to make good on the promise that God's end-time rule will break in. Jesus' resurrection is the 'first-fruits' (I Cor. 15: 20, 23) of the end time, the inauguration though not the full actualization, of the eschatological new creation ... It promises new life out of living death". (Kelsey *op.cit* p.79).

This promise means that, post-resurrection, death can never again have the last word – and neither can those living deaths which people find themselves having to undergo yet for which the "consolations of religion" have but little to offer them. But when such afflicted people have faith in God's promise and its fulfilment now, though not fully yet, in the dire depths of their present situation then they can see, even through their tears, that this suffering comes vouchsaving Hope – and therein there is redemption.

Redemption is my Desert Island Doctrine. It seems to me that it pre-supposes and fulfils all that Christianity essentially professes and proclaims. Yet it is not a doctrine which is served well by the prescriptive and propositional requirements of a religious system. Whilst religion has shown an almost promiscuous interest in how individual or even corporate sinners can be put right with God, so many theories of atonement do little or nothing to foster hope of redemption in the hearts and minds of those who have good reason to think of themselves as victims rather than vicious.

Redemption is not so much a religious transaction as an effusion of faith. It is by faith in the presence, love and faithfulness of God that redemption can be realised, even in the very depths of suffering, as the in-breaking of God's new creation holding out hope for life in all its fullness and making good on God's promise to make all things new. Suddenly religion seems altogether too pre-occupied with its own petty agendas to deliver on this vision which is surely God's agenda for all who turn to Him in faith.

It is noticeable that "redemption" rarely features as a separate entry in theological dictionaries and introductions. It is usually subsumed under "atonement" or "salvation". Adrian Hastings' *Oxford Companion to Christian Thought* is a notable exception. Failure to give redemption its proper due results both from suspicion as to its somewhat unsavoury origins so that it becomes guilty by association with illiberal practices, and also from a tendency to see redemption almost exclusively in terms of individualistic and legalistic categories. Therefore it is important to rescue redemption from its bondage to religion and release it into the realms of faith, where what is on offer is not subscription to a verbal contract but the prospect of a leap of faith into the promised land of God's presence, peace and power of love. In that sense redemption itself cries out to be redeemed.

No End of Faith

When it comes to a biblical word-count in the encounter between faith and religion, there is effectively no contest. Not only does "faith" occur hundreds of times more often than "religion" in the English translations, but this also reflects the rarity value of religion as a concept in both the Hebrew and Greek scriptures as a whole. In Acts 26 vs 5 and James 1 vs 26 the Greek word *threskeia* is commonly translated "religion" and refers to the cultus as a system of worship rather than to beliefs or codes of conduct. This word is also used by Paul at Colossians 2 vs 18 to describe cultic-worship practices. This underlines that the concept of religion does not sit comfortably with biblical thought and so is rarely found.

However, as we have seen, there is a good deal of subtlety to be appreciated in the ways in which words for faith are used in the Bible and this applies particularly to the shades of meaning associated with the Hebrew *emunah* and the Greek *pistis*. We have suggested, following Frost and Hirsch, that *pistis* accommodates itself to the categories of religion rather more readily than does the Hebrew word so that even if "religion" as a word occurs relatively rarely in the Bible, still its core categories and associations are present in some of the ways in which faith is intended to be interpreted and understood. F. D. Grealy almost certainly overstates the case when he suggests that "the primary importance of the term 'religion' in the New Testament is in its pointing to the shift that was taking place in the Hellenistic Churches from the Hebrew understanding of faith as concrete obedience of the whole man (sic) to God, to faith as an ecclesiastically approved system of doctrine, worship and behaviour" – but he does have a point (*The Interpreters Dictionary of the Bible* Vo 4 p.32).

A major focus of New Testament Studies in the era of historical criticism has been upon how the emergence of a network of Churches in the earliest Christian decades impacted upon the form, content and purpose of what became the books of the New Testament. The precise nature and extent of any such influence will continue to be hotly debated, but it is reasonable to assume that how the early Church told and re-told the story of its Founder and the origins of its own corporate life and worship must have been significantly affected by its emerging perceptions and priorities. Furthermore, it is reasonable to assume that these perceptions and priorities would have been coloured above all by the need to establish a clear sense of identity, doctrine and discipline in a cultural context of incomprehension and frequent hostility. These are what we have come to think of as characteristically religious concerns which, at their best, are necessary to the effective protection and propagation of faith, but which can so easily become ends in themselves and so end up as masters rather than servants of the faith which inspired them.

Tracing such influences is clearly of greatest interest to students of the four Gospels, and we could choose virtually at random to illustrate how religious imperatives might have impacted upon the seminal narratives recounting the life and death of Jesus of Nazareth. For example, to what extent do the Infancy or Passion Narratives reflect the liturgical patterns beginning to take hold in fledgling Christian communities? To what extent does the material peculiar to Luke on the one hand, and Matthew on the other, reflect the socio-religious profile of their respective audiences? To what extent do the initiation and Eucharistic practices of the earliest congregations inform the accounts of the Ethiopian eunuch, the road to Emmaus, the Last Supper and the miraculous feedings of the multitudes? And having mentioned the road to Emmaus, to what extent does the need to clarify the leadership role of Peter or the role of Mary or of women generally in the early Church, find expression in the Resurrection narratives? Indeed, these narratives at the end of the Gospels might be as good a point as any from which to view the early influence of religion upon Easter faith and the formulation of its written record.

***

"There are only six stories in the history of the world, and they are all in the Soaps and they are all in the Bible".

The press conference called to announce my appointment as a Diocesan Bishop was following a pretty predictable pattern until I was asked which TV programmes I made a point of watching. "Eastenders", I replied, "I've never knowingly missed an episode". Of course, interest levels on the part of the assembled media rose instantly, and on being asked why I was an Eastenders fan I gave the above response. One national newspaper featured it as one of their "Ten Top Quotes of the Year" – though I suspect more out of curiosity than conviction! The next step was to try and justify this off the top of the head remark and, in fact, it proved remarkably easy to substantiate. It also led me to reflect further on Soaps as a genre of narrative drama with clear and close correlations to the kind of story-telling found in the Bible, and particularly in the Gospels. This impression was confirmed a couple of years later by Morna D. Hooker in her book *Endings: Invitations to Discipleship* (SCM 2003). She shows how there is an element of open-endedness about the endings of many or even most books of the Old Testament. "Almost all our Old Testament books have conclusions that look forward to what is going to happen next" she writes (p 10), and we are immediately reminded of the cliff-hanger device which leaves Soap viewers up in the air and waiting impatiently for the next episode. Whilst people tend to be irritated by novels and plays which fail to achieve closure by neatly tying up the loose ends (see Frank Kermode: *The Sense of an Ending* OUP 1967 p.19), this lack of a definitive resolution is what people expect of a Soap, and it defines its character.

So what about the Gospels? To what extent do they share this particular characteristic? What about their endings? This is the question to which Morna Hooker addresses herself and her general conclusion is that, indeed, all four Gospels end by looking forward to what comes next and therefore have "suspended endings". She argues that "each of our authors invites the members of his audience to take up the story and write the final scene of the drama for themselves" (p. 82). However, she does have to qualify this general observation when it comes to the Fourth Gospel because "for John, it would seem that Jesus' exaltation on the cross is the end of the story ... with his death, all things are completed" (p. 83).

In other words, St. John's Gospel is not much of a cliff-hanger. In fact the final cry of Jesus from the Cross – "it is finished!" – is about as decisive as any narrator could make it, and the subsequent resurrection narrative is but the triumphant confirmation of a victory already secured. In St. John's account, Jesus remains firmly in control right to the end. All loose ends are tied up, wrongs are righted – especially in relation to Peter's denials and Thomas' doubts – and the past where sin and Satan once ruled and people once dead stayed dead is now itself dead and buried. A new day has dawned, a new world has been created, everything is done and dusted – a perfect ending. Or what in musical circles would be called a Perfect Cadence.

In fact the variety of cadences used to end pieces of music can help to illustrate the different endings to our four Gospels. If John provides a Perfect Cadence to round off his Gospel in a way that is satisfyingly conclusive, the same may not be said for Matthew and Luke and certainly cannot be said of Mark's ending.

For Matthew, the Resurrection represents the dramatic in-breaking of the Kingdom of Heaven. A decisive battle against sin and death has been fought and won, but the war goes on. We who would be followers of Christ are commissioned to go on fighting for good against evil, for right against wrong. For Matthew the

Resurrection is not so much an end, as the beginning – the beginning of the End. The battle cry is "Onward Christian Soldiers", and do not rest until the new world order inaugurated by the Resurrection of Jesus has become a reality for all people everywhere. What Matthew provides by way of an ending is what is called an "Interrupted" or "Suspended" Cadence which leaves the listener waiting for the resolution of what is otherwise still unresolved – the end is now, but not yet.

For Luke, the Resurrection is likewise a Suspended Cadence. The risen Jesus points the way forward for his Disciples, and Luke's second volume describes the acts of the Apostles as they take forward his mission "throughout all Judea and Samaria, and even in the farthest corners of the earth" (Acts 1 vs 8). For Luke the Resurrection is not so much the end, or the beginning of the end, but the end of the beginning. There is more work to be done and, as Disciples of Christ, we are the ones to do it. We are empowered and emboldened by the Resurrection to work God's will in the world because we know that never again will evil and death have the last word. For Luke, as for Matthew, the Resurrection signifies unfinished business – work in progress.

However, for all the dramatic power and intensity evident in the Gospel endings crafted by John, Matthew and Luke it is Mark's telling of the Resurrection story which is the most remarkable. After the women find the tomb empty, and are told by the young man inside the tomb that Jesus has been raised, he has gone ahead of them to Galilee, and they must tell this to Peter and the other Disciples, Mark simply reports that "they went out and ran away from the tomb, trembling with amazement. They said nothing to anyone, for they were afraid" (Mark 16 vs 8).

There his Gospel comes to an abrupt halt. From quite early times efforts were made to provide what people thought would be a proper ending, with an extension to verse 8 and/or additional verses 9 – 20 being provided in some versions. But the style of these additions is clearly at odds with the rest of the

Gospel, and they simply attempt to summarise what is found elsewhere. So there can be little doubt that Mark intended to leave us with those women awestruck, terrified and fleeing away. Somehow, what they had seen and heard was just too hot to handle. They knew the world as it was where sin and evil held sway, and dead people stayed dead, and they had sort of learned to live with it, to accommodate it, to compromise with it. But this news of a risen Lord was overwhelming. They were not brave enough for this brave new world, and Mark leaves them and us in a state of fear and trembling. For Mark, the Resurrection as the end of the Jesus story signals no end of trouble for those who dare to follow him. This is most definitely a cliff-hanger of an ending for which the musical equivalent will be a very scary cadence indeed.

Francis J. Maloney describes how the woman ran away from the tomb "associating themselves with the fear, trembling, astonishment and flight of the disciples" (see Mark 14 vss 50 – 52) (Francis J. Maloney: *Mark – Storyteller, Interpreter, Evangelist* Hendrickson 2004 p. 112). For Maloney, as for many other commentators, the theme of failure is key to understanding Mark's Gospel. The Cross is communicated as an apparent failure of Jesus' mission which, like him, hangs there abandoned and aborted. The disciples are regularly portrayed as failing to understand his message and they prove frail and fragile in the face of dangers and temptations. It would appear that God took enormous risks in the act of Incarnation, and Jesus likewise took risks when it came to recruiting disciples and retaining them. Somehow, there is little in all of this to make us feel that it has much to do with religion which we generally experience as risk-averse, allergic to failure and routinely robust in recruiting its representatives. But it is strong on faith – faith in God's promises which are never found to fail notwithstanding the fears and failures of those called to follow Him. This is why Mark is able to end his Gospel as he does. The disciples know, and Mark's readers know, that throughout his journeying with them Jesus' promises always come true and, of course, the most important of these promises related to his death and resurrection (Mark 8 vs 31; 9 vs 31; 10 vss 33 – 34). This being so, Mark's readers have every reason to believe that the promises found in Mark 14 vs 28 and 16 vs 7 about meeting the disciples in Galilee after the Resurrection must have been fulfilled so that the fear which overcame the women was itself overcome by the faith which God's promises inspire. Fear and failure redeemed through faith is truly good news for those who first read Mark's Gospel, and remains good news for all who read Mark's Gospel today.

By comparison, for all that Matthew and Luke have "suspended endings" which look forward to what comes next, there is that about the future which is significantly more prescriptive than anything to be found in Mark 16. The final verses of Matthew's Gospel possibly capture something of the flavour of the official decree of Cyrus of Persia in II Chronicles 36 vs 23, which is particularly significant given that II Chronicles was the very last book in the Hebrew scriptures. Matthew 28 vss 18 – 20 certainly has the feel of a religious injunction which fulfils in a thoroughly Christological and Trinitarian way the purposes of God entrusted to disciples, and then to a Church, by Him to whom "full authority in heaven and earth has been committed". Whilst Luke's commissioning of the disciples has rather less of an "ecclesiastical" feel to it, still we sense that we are in the realms of religion with a clear job description and direction of travel determining matters of membership, leadership, discipline and doctrine for the fledgling Christian community.

Richard Burridge says of St. John's Gospel that "the resurrection story ... (brings) about the climax and closure of the whole story" (*Four Gospels, One Jesus?* SPCK 1994 p.159). It would be difficult to use the word "closure" to describe the endings of any of the other Gospels and this means that the Fourth Gospel has in this respect, as in many others, a character all its own. The matter is complicated by uncertainties as to the provenance of Chapter 21. Morna Hooker asks why this chapter might have been added, and offers several possibilities:

"Was it just to rehabilitate Peter? Was it because the author had heard these stories from other Christians, and wished to incorporate them into this book? Was it because he felt the need to include a command to the disciples to evangelize the nations? Or did he perhaps decide that the original ending of the Gospel had not been sufficiently open-ended, and that the Christian community had to be reminded that they had a task to do? Certainly the significance of Jesus' commission to the disciples is underlined in these final lines". (*op.cit* pp. 79 – 80).

Whatever the reason or reasons may have been, we are confirmed in our impression that the Gospel of John as contained in Chapters 1 – 20 is the least "open-ended" of the Gospels, with Jesus portrayed as a controlling figure who has accomplished the work of salvation for which he came into the world so that he now returns to the Father, leaving behind him those who will live in his light, walk in his way and enter into that place which he has prepared for all who trust in him.

For all its spiritual depth, theological sophistication and undoubted beauty, St. John's Gospel does have an "all or nothing" feel to it which tends to characterise religious commitments rather than acts of faith. Whatever the nature and extent of "the Johannine Circle", the fact that such a designation is plausible underlines the distinctiveness of John's Gospel and its disposition to define a group in ways associated more with determining religious affiliation than describing personal faith.

It is generally agreed that Mark's Gospel was the first to be written, and so we are left to ponder upon how quickly accounts of Jesus' Resurrection moved from his emphasis on faith through fear and failure to the recruitment of Resurrection narratives to serve a rather more religious prospectus. It seems to have happened quite quickly if the Gospels of Matthew, Luke and John are our guides in this respect and this suggests that faith has always been fighting a losing battle against the regulatory and systematizing tendencies of religion. That there have been those throughout history who have resolutely resisted such tendencies, often running the risk of heresy trials in the process, does not detract from the need for vigilance lest religion become the master rather than the servant of faith – including faith in Resurrection itself.

In *Easter Faith* (DLT 2003 p. 107), Gerald O'Collins writes:

"Undoubtedly, Easter faith makes striking demands on believers. Yet any cost can be cheerfully borne. That is because such faith responds to the good news of the risen Christ, as Ludwig Wittgenstein put it, 'believingly – i.e. lovingly'. 'It is *love*', he continued, 'that believes the Resurrection'."

Somehow the language of love, even tough love, struggles with the all too prevalent view of religion as prescriptive, restrictive, doleful and even hateful. Rescuing Resurrection from abuse by religion might just liberate it to speak the language of love to a world in which religious hatred speaks loudest and lives longest in memory and imagination.

O'Collins also cites the case of the Revd. Ernest Pontifex in Samuel Butler's novel *The Way of all Flesh*. He is challenged by a non-believing tinker to give him the story of the Resurrection told by St. John. However, Pontifex only succeeds in mixing up the Easter narratives from the four Gospels so that the tinker finds it easy to point out inaccuracies and inconsistencies. This prompts Pontifex to attempt to bring the four versions into a "tolerable harmony with each other" and when he signally fails to do so he abandons his faith in Christ risen from the dead. As O'Collins points out, poor Pontifex had crudely misrepresented the nature of the Gospel narratives which should be read prayerfully and with a sensitivity to their spiritual message:

"Like those who hear poetry, visit art exhibitions, attend concerts, and go to the theatre, readers of the Gospels must be guided not by artificial procedures and rigid pedantry but by passionate engagement and the deep concerns of the heart. Then even more than those who open themselves to the beauty of literature, art, music and drama, they will catch the deft touches, personal insights and enriching variations with which the four evangelists tell the sublime story of Jesus' dying and rising into glory". (*The Tablet* April 2000, p. 552).

Quite so, but only so long as it is acknowledged that as with art, music, poetry and drama the "deft touches" and "personal insights" may not always be "enriching". Whilst we would not wish to be without the Resurrection narratives as recounted by Matthew, Luke and John, we are still entitled to have a view as to whether they have enriched Mark's fearful, faith-filled account or somehow detracted from it with their rather more expansive excursions into a mystery more conducive to Mark's open-ended and open-hearted minimalism. For example, the sacramental symbolism of the Road to Emmaus holds religious resonances which are deeply moving and re-assuring, but surely they are far less challenging to faith and discipleship than a flight from an empty tomb with the words "He has been raised" ringing in your ears!

No Faith in the Church?

"Trying to take a long view of the Church I have been struck by the fact that, looking back, the out-standing achievements are almost invariably the fruit of imagination, courage and clear-headed intelligence, whereas the failures are about insensitivity, refusal to face conflict, fear of what religions extremists or the press will say, or sheer woolly-headedness and fudge". (Monica Furlong).

On 16th April 2006 the New York Times carried an article entitled *Christianity, The Brand*. It was a profile of Larry Ross, a highly successful marketing executive, who helped to turn religious public relations into big business in America. The inexorable rise of "The Brand" in the worlds of marketing and advertising has been well documented (see especially Naomi Klein's *No Logo*) and its chief object and effect is to distract consumers from the quality of the product itself so that what attracts them, and motivates them to make a purchase, is the brand name or logo which has impacted sufficiently on their consciousness to make the product feel good and right for them irrespective of whether it is best value for money. Benjamin R. Barber has traced the rise of The Brand (see *Consumed* Norton Press 2007 pp. 166 – 213) in a chilling account of how the public in the developed world has become infantilized by marketing techniques which manipulate purchasing decisions so that they are more about buying into a branded lifestyle rather than making deliberate choices about the qualities of a product and their fitness for purpose. The product itself is now a second order issue: the first order issue is to do with what the brand name promises when it comes to what owning this particular product says to us and to others about who we are and our place in the firmament of fashion and fad.

So is Christianity a brand? Or, put more generally, is religion an exercise in branding faith so that buying into a particular religious brand becomes more important than the faith it purports to promote? If, as such luminaries as R. H. Tawney, Max Weber and Karl Marx have argued, capitalism has been parasitic upon religion in general and Protestantism in particular, then might not the emergence of "the brand" in contemporary capitalism be likewise parasitic upon how religion "branded" Christian faith so that buying into the brand has become more important than the character and quality of the faith contained in the religious packaging. Kierkegaard observed that at the first Christmas God gave humankind a present, and whereas usually the first thing we do with a present is unwrap it, the fact is that in relation to this particular present we have spent 2,000 years wrapping it up.

Perhaps Christendom has itself been the market leader when it comes to branding faith so that adherents buy into a denominational (Roman Catholic), national (Church of England) or cultural brand rather than consciously embracing the faith from which they have been distracted by the religious packaging. This could be described as belonging without believing – belonging to the community of the brand matters more than being committed to the faith "product" which the religious "brand" purports to promote but which it effectively replaces in the hearts and minds of the "consumers". Certainly the world of marketing has not been slow to hijack religious categories "for the creation of brand worship [so that] brands are the new religion" (Douglas Atkin *The Culting of Brands: When Customers Become True Believers*. New York: Portfolio 2004 p xi) – and religious groups have been far from averse to using current marketing techniques to "sell" their message. So there is clearly a case to be made for seeing some synergy between the marketing of a brand at the expense of the product, and the propagating of religion at the expense of faith.

Is a box of chocolates a box with chocolates in, or chocolates in a box? It depends! If I am buying hand-made Belgian chocolates for my wife then I go to a specialist purveyor of fine chocolates and point out to the assistant from the selection on offer the precise chocolates I want to purchase. These are then placed in a plain box and I have to pay extra to have them gift wrapped. The choice of the individual chocolates matters more than the attractiveness of the box they come in. On the other hand, if I am on my way to a dinner party and I want to take chocolates as a gift for my host, I am likely to choose the best-looking box with little thought for the chocolates inside, as I want to make a good impression when handing them over and, anyway, I know nothing of my host's particular tastes or preferences. Perhaps faith is more about the contents of the box whilst religion is more to do with the packaging which would, of course, represent the ultimate triumph of image over substance. This triumph is one of the best recorded, and most derided, aspects of contemporary culture, and is assumed to be a by-product of modernity as it has evolved over the past four hundred years or so. Yet it may well have roots which lie deep in the origins of Christianity as a religion traceable to Jesus of Nazareth but owing more to the emergence of the Christian Church as a brand rather than the intentions of the One from whom it takes its name.

We have already suggested that moves towards giving the story of Jesus a rather more "religious" aspect, as distinct from a faith-focussed orientation, began with accounts of the Resurrection which was, of course, the seminal event which gave to the followers of the Way their distinctive character and motivation. Mark's version of events on the first Easter Day offers a great deal to inspire faith in the face of fear and uncertainty, whilst the other Evangelists invest their narratives of the post-Resurrection appearances with significant details and symbolic references which can readily be seem as the calling cards of an incipient religion.

Furthermore, what applies to the Resurrection narratives

characterises the overall impression given by the Gospels as a whole. So Leslie Houlden, having reminded us of how unedifying is the picture given in Mark of the Disciples as "blunderers, failures, and traitors, as hopeless as "followers" and as models for the Church" concludes that "for Mark, Jesus was little concerned to do anything that one could call 'founding the Church'". (*Jesus*. Continuum 2003 p. 180). Meanwhile, Houlden suggests that Matthew "is less problematic in this regard". He is "the practical Churchman, providing for the community's role in the guidance and discipline of its members". Matthew's view of Christian life was "firmly institutional, and his Jesus is a provider of structure for his followers" (p. 181). Likewise Luke, though more in Acts than in the Gospel, was most concerned "to heal the major rift in early Christianity between the Pauline mission ('liberal' in its terms of admission of Gentiles) and the less indulgent (and less imaginative?) Jewish – Christians centered (until A.D.70) on the Jerusalem Church". In other words, issues of leadership, membership and discipline were significant Lukan concerns so that Mark's "followers" (of Jesus) are beginning to look more like "members" (of a movement) and, when we come to Johannine Christianity, they are very clearly a part of, or apart from, a circle "exposed to some of the meaner aspects of church life: power struggles and squabbles – to-the-death about the formulation of belief" (p. 182).

Of course, it is to St. Paul that we must look for the earliest application of the Greek word "*ekklesia*" to describe the corporate expression of Christianity. Whilst we must beware of reading too many nuances into Paul's usage, it is clear that he took a concept well established in civic / faith community contexts to mean a calling together of citizens / God's people for a common purpose, and adapted it to convey the shared life of worship and witness appropriate to those who are "in Christ". Whilst this sense of being in a mystical communion with Christ remained crucial for Paul, and is at least implicit in what he means by *ekklesia* in e.g. I

Corinthians 10 vs 32; 12 vs 28 and Philippians 3 vs 6, we are alert to ways in which he earths the word so as to refer to assemblies of Christians in specific places. In the case of the Thessalonians (I Thes 1 vs 1 and II Thes 1 vs 1) there is a sense in which it is the faithful more or less independent of the context in which they are set which is being referred to (a gathered Church?) whereas in Romans 16 vs 1, I Corinthians 1 vs 2 and Galatians 1 vs 2 it matters that they are where they are rather than somewhere else (a communal Church?).

In any case, Paul never loses sight of the Christian Church as essentially the new Israel destined to fulfil what the Scriptures proclaimed to be the destiny of God's chosen people. So *ekklesia* is a thoroughly religious notion insofar as it is about defining and, to some extent, limiting the provenance and privileges of those who are "in *ekklesia*" – very much what we mean by "in Church" apart from the fact that he does not think of a special building (see C. K. Barrett: *Paul*. Geoffrey Chapman 1994 p. 121).

So whilst Paul's understanding of *ekklesia* is essentially predicated upon the people of God "in Christ" as the Body of Christ and the New Israel, a people united in the faith into which they were baptised, he cannot escape the challenges consequent upon having to give corporate expression to such personal faith in the context of day-to-day realities. As John Ziesler puts it "this future people lives within the present doomed world, and therefore needs its own structures and ministries" (*Pauline Christianity*. OUP 1983 p. 68). In Paul's time these were pretty ill-defined with Christians assembling in private houses to participate in unplanned or even, in the case of Corinth, chaotic worship led by members who held no clearly defined office but upon whom the power of the Spirit was believed to have alighted for just that occasion. Ziesler concludes that "Paul is more interested in the Church's place in God's pattern of salvation than in its organisation".

Notwithstanding this relative indifference to ecclesiastical structures, driven no doubt by the imperatives of firm faith and world-renouncing discipleship as the end-time drew near, still we detect seeds being sown which in the next generation would see growth in the infrastructure of faith – and the roots of religion.

Yet it took time, and Rowan Williams has written movingly about how concerns to define, protect and enforce the purity and sacredness of the *ekklesia* well into the post-Apostolic era were motivated not by institutional drivers but by the need to preserve the identity of the Church as "resident aliens" with the *Letter to Diognetus* and the martyrdom of Polycarp being key indicators of what mattered to them most (*Why Study the Past?* DLT 2005). It is this same concern for what Williams calls "independent citizenship" which undergirds the "obsessive interest in doctrinal correctness" (*op.cit* p. 48) in the early Christian centuries. Readiness for martyrdom goes to the heart of Christian distinctiveness in this period, and Williams sees this re-surfacing throughout Church history so that, for example, when in 1936 the Confessing Church in Germany issued the Barmen Declaration affirming the sovereignty of God over all other claims to authority, "the primitive shape of Christian self-definition became visible once more" (*op.cit*. p. 54). Indeed, it is worth noting that the Greek word *paroikos*, which translates as "resident alien" in I Peter 2 vs 11, is the root of our words parish and parochial. Such is the persistence of this idea through history, and it may have done as much as anything to try and ensure that the distinctiveness of the Church as a faith community does not get sacrificed on the altar of religious institutionalism, whereby systemic conformity comes to matter more than Christlike trust in the truth that makes us free, but which may cost us everything.

We are glad and grateful for the persistence of this theme with its challenges to cheap grace and to the easy assimilation of Christianity into the socio-political categories of the prevailing culture. We are also glad and grateful that the Church at its best has been the guarantor of God's good news as both a gift and a goad to individuals and communities to such good effect. Yet the early pressure to structure, dogmatize and discipline faith in Christ has never relented, neither has the tendency to "brand" such faith in the livery of ecclesiastical enterprises. If Christianity is not itself a brand, what has been called "Churchianity" most certainly is. Remember that branding effectively puts the packaging ahead of the product for presentational and promotional purposes, and as soon as issues to do with the structure and organisation of the Church began to assume an ever greater profile then the trend towards branding the faith of Christians was likely to prove unstoppable.

It cannot be underlined too often that there is nothing in the nature and purpose of ecclesiastical organisation itself that is inconsistent with the expression and propagation of the Gospel. In fact, as the end-time which had been anticipated imminently, receded into a more open-ended future, the development of formal provision for organisation and oversight of the Body of Christ became not only inevitable but absolutely essential. But with it came the temptation which beguiles all organisations when their ways and means become more important than their ends and objects. Rowan Williams has shown how the early Church resisted that temptation rather longer, and with greater success than might have been expected, but by the fourth Century the Christian Church had a brand profile which even the Emperor could not resist. Controversy will continue to rage as to the circumstances pertaining to Constantine's "conversion", but it is pertinent to ask whether the sign of the Cross which appeared to him at the Milvian Bridge in 312 A.D. heralded victory for faith in Christ or the triumph of the Church's logo. Either way, the power of the Church assumed proportions which could never have been envisaged by those "resident aliens" for whom their *ekklesia* was a counter-cultural assembly for worship, teaching and mutual encouragement rather than an enterprise available to be recruited for all kinds of social, economic and political purposes. The box containing the chocolates had come to matter more than the chocolates in the box. The fires of Pentecostal faith were now brought under control by the priorities of power and the promotion of ecclesiastical brands which would come to dominate European culture for nigh on two thousand years. Martyn Percy has provided a particularly challenging account of how power is used and abused in ecclesiastical contexts, and especially in fundamentalist and charismatic groups (*Power and the Church*. Cassell 1998). The rise of religion at the expense of faith represents one of the most remarkable yet regrettable trajectories of the Common Era.

At this point we do well to stop and take stock lest we descend into the rhetoric of a rant. As so often Rowan Williams puts our anxieties into a proper perspective:

"The Church's self-definition *matters*. To be clear about the Church's boundaries can become an obsessive concern with knowing who is outside, who can be trusted to reflect orthodoxy as I have learned it. But definition matters, ultimately, so that resistance is possible to the idolatrous claims of total power that may be made from time to time in the world. Definition matters so that the Christian is free to say with conviction that the truth of the world and of humanity is not at the disposal of this or that system of political management ... Inevitably, the Church becomes involved in patrolling its boundaries; not every spirit is of Christ, not every way of speaking and acting is capable of being transparent to Christ. Discipline is exercised, so that what is said and done in the Church displays its accountability".

Here Williams addresses several of those elements of ecclesiastical life which we have invoked as being at least guilty by association with the aberrancies of religion. Issues to do with who's in and who's out; who's qualified to teach the Truth and who isn't; what can be legitimately asserted and what cannot; what words or deeds might require discipline and who might administer it with appropriate authority – all these we have identified as features of a faith to some extent subverted by the regulatory rigours of religion. But significantly he sees these features as crucial to ensuring that faith in Christ "is not at the disposal of this or that system of political management". In other words, these structural provisions have as their justification clarity of self-definition in order to deter the recruitment of God to serve socio-political agendas which we have seen as characteristic of religion. The features of religion are therefore seen as at the service of a distinctive faith which needs to be carefully policed and patrolled precisely to preserve its "resident alien" status and integrity.

However, Williams offers his own caveat: "But when all justice has been done to this need, an area of reserve remains: we do not yet know what will be drawn out of us by the pressure of Christ's reality, what the full shape of a future orthodoxy might be" (*loc.cit.*). This is a crucial point which experience suggests is more than merely "an area of reserve". How often have new insights and opportunities "drawn out of us by the pressure of Christ's reality" been stifled by the counter-pressures of religio-political conformity? For example, although the Reformers sought to recover the understanding of faith as trust in the redemptive initiative and action of God, in reaction to the religious excesses and abuses of the medieval Church, it is not difficult to identify the points at which Protestantism left itself open to being colonised by economic and political causes, and Protestant Churches came to display more and more that obsession with certainty and authenticity which feeds religious exclusiveness and bigotry. Likewise, for all the idealism and evangelistic zeal of the earliest overseas mission initiatives, it was not long before religiously motivated rivalries were exported and entrenched. Whilst Kevin Ward demonstrates how local agency and creativity played a significant part in how Christianity was received and expressed in countries subject to

Anglican missionary activities "in liturgy and architecture, in styles of theology and discipleship, and not least in its relation to secular power, Anglicanism ... often reflected, all too closely, its cultural origins" (*A History of Global Anglicanism* CUP 2006 p. 16). Somehow it is difficult not to think that the way in which Rwanda, one of the most quickly Christianised countries in Africa, descended so quickly into genocidal anarchy suggests a veneer of religious affiliation rather than a deeply rooted trust in the Lordship of Christ. Finally, the commodification of faith as evidenced in a great deal of contemporary Christianity and catalogued by John Drane in *The McDonaldization of the Church* (DLT 2000) further illustrates how the cosmetics of religious branding compromise faithfulness to the gracious initiative of God in Christ.

These examples, and others, give little cause for comfort that faith can rely on religion to serve its purposes rather than colluding with a culture of pre-packaged and non-negotiable nostrums waiting to be embraced by a range of dubious patrons. John Brenkman has coined the intriguing phrase "entrepreneurs of the soul" to describe those who appropriate facets of Christianity and Islam for political purposes and, of course, he could have included socio-economic purposes as well. (*The Cultural Contradictions of Democracy: Political Thought Since September 11*, Princeton 2007). This is a great challenge to the Churches, which have to live creatively into the tension between faith and religion at a time when their fortunes are at a relatively low ebb in the erstwhile citadels of Christendom. To that challenge we now turn.

We have seen how for Bonhoeffer "religionless Christianity" was most appropriate for humanity "come of age", and for Kierkegaard an immediate religiousness which removed the Church from the path of the Individual on the verge of a "leap of faith" corresponded most closely to New Testament Christianity. Yet for neither of them was the Church rendered redundant. It was a matter of re-dressing an imbalance – what Kierkegaard described as providing a "corrective" – in the relationship between religion and faith. We have seen how the origins of this tension can be traced back to the pages of the New Testament, and we have also shown how the redressing of such an imbalance works out in relation to doctrine in general, but to the doctrine of redemption in particular. It is not about eradicating religion in order to secure once and for all the priority of faith. We misunderstand Luther, for example, if we see this as being the sum of his protest against the Catholic Church. Rather, it is about securing the priority of faith as trust in God's prevenient grace by ensuring that religious observances and obligations are always at the service of Christian individuals and communities so as to assist in expressing and celebrating their faith rather than seeking to determine and define it.

So what is entailed for the Church in achieving the appropriate balance between faith and religion?

For a start, it will entail the Church locally, nationally and globally being clear about what it is for, and what it is not for. It is possible to envisage a spectrum of possibilities from Church as agent of religion and enemy of faith to Church as friendly to faith and hostile to religion. Where a Church positions itself on such a spectrum will be indicated by a number of attitudes and assumptions which ultimately determine policies and decisions.

For example, a Church perceiving itself to be the agent of religion will have strict border controls which exist not so much to preserve its distinctiveness as to deter potential polluters. Because of its confidence in the certainty and non-negotiability of its beliefs and praxis it will have a great deal to say to others about their outlooks and lifestyles and spend relatively little time reviewing its own credentials. It will have relatively little time for the faith of others unless and until that faith has come to conform to their own pre-packaged criteria for doctrinal correctness and ethical conformity. Such a Church has little faith in God to be busy about God's work of re-creation, redemption and revelation in the life of the world and the lives of those who may not describe themselves as religious, but for whom God still has meaning and significance. In such a Church the good news of God needs to be guarded and protected in a gated ghetto of religious conformity lest it prove too fragile to withstand the rigours of robust debate or even open hostility. It will have little truck with H. L. Mencken's maxim that "for every difficult and complex problem, there is a solution which is simple, straight-forward – and wrong!". For those who muster under the banner of religion, the things of God are seldom difficult or complex, and the Gospel is essentially simple, straightforward and right. This is a Church which crucially sees itself as guarding the base-camp of received teachings and traditions – a very necessary and important task – but without any real sense of the base-camp being guarded so as to allow others to probe the perimeter fence of religious orthodoxy and thereby pioneer risky but faith-fuelled forays into God's future which may well prove to be another country with untold riches yet to be revealed. This will be a Church which is more prescriptive than prophetic, more about dogmatism than dialogue, exposition than exploration, certainty than searching. It is more likely to be legislating against than liberating for – and pastoring will be more to do with discipline than the gentler arts of compassion and persuasion.

On the other hand, a Church at the other end of the spectrum will have little patience with anything which remotely resonates with the trappings of religion. There will be a suspicion of doctrinal statements which require assent before membership can be granted. Indeed, membership itself will be viewed with great suspicion because of its exclusivist tendencies, and radical creativity will be at a premium in a Church allergic to any kind of credal confidence. It will put tolerance at the top of its list of essential self-defining characteristics, yet be pathologically intolerant of anyone who thinks anything is essential in the free-for-all of faith. It will tend towards the post-modern mantra that it doesn't matter what you believe, so long as you believe that it doesn't matter, with its consequential emphasis on how rather than what people believe. It will celebrate the multi-faceted mystery of God, and remain deeply suspicious of prescribed rites and rituals which are seen more as gatekeepers of cultic orthodoxy than gateways to liturgical imagination. It will see Jesus more as a brother in solidarity with the human condition than as any kind of divine intermediary achieving for humanity what humanity could achieve for itself if left alone by religion to realise its full potential. In fact religion and superstition would be seen as all of a piece, because they both corrupt the human commitment to have faith in humanity and in God as the ultimate realisation of human fulfilment. So it will be a Church where what is possible is more important than what is believed to be the case; where what is received from the past as true must pass through quality control policed by personal preferences and experience; where all truth-claims are provisional (except for that one!); where the wisdom of the ages must answer at the bar of modern knowledge and most likely to be found wanting; where all attempts to institutionalise, professionalize or regularise the things that belong to faith must be actively resisted and roundly condemned.

Somewhere, surely, between those extremes there is a Church where faith and religion can co-exist in a mutually enriching relationship. Enough has been said so far for it to be clear that such a point on the spectrum is likely to be more towards the faith-friendly than the agent-of-religion extreme. This is necessary to provide a corrective to the resurgence of religion in a world where there is not nearly enough faith. It is also necessary because the counter-cultural character of Christianity is all too easily compromised by denominational "branding" and susceptibility to endorsement by those whose motives may at best be mixed.

What might such a Church look like? First of all, it will see boundaries not as barriers but as meeting places, and will incline towards hospitality rather than hostility when it comes to those who see things differently and behave accordingly. Crucially it will be a Church where religion as requisite and necessary to its stability and integrity will only ever be at the service of faith, and will never become an end in itself. The faith-fascists who have no tolerance at all for the role of religion in ecclesiastical ecology do little to further the Christian cause in contemporary culture. Whilst they are content to assume the mantle of forward-facing pioneers pressing on beyond the perimeter fence of Tradition to explore the far country armed with the ordnance of reason and experience, they tend to forget that they can only do this because of those who guard the base-camp of scriptural revelation and theological insights which have got the pioneers this far and which resource their ventures into the future. The base-camp keepers must remember that one of the main reasons for guarding the base-camp is to facilitate that pioneering spirit which is essential to a faith which is living and not dead. But, for their part, the risk taking faith-filled pioneers must acknowledge that without the base-camp keepers their mission would be impossible.

So we are on the watch for a Church which is founded upon trust in the creative, redemptive and sanctifying initiative of God, incarnate in Jesus, and effective through the power of the Holy Spirit. This is the faith which is God's gift to a pilgrim people communicated through revelation, tradition, reason and experience yet never fully comprehended by even the most sophisticated or subtle manifestations of religion. This is the faith we celebrate in worship when we honour God with our praises and entrust God with our prayers; it is the faith we seek to share by word and example with those who share with us the journey of life; it is the faith which forms us into a fellowship with those who share the gift, and the faith which fosters fellow-feeling with those who most need to experience such selfless love as is faith's truest expression. It is the faith which arouses in us righteous indignation in the face of cruelty, greed, discrimination and injustice. It is the faith which emboldens us to protest and prophesy against the abuses of power and privilege which corrupt the goodness of God's creation and hold in contempt the image of God in which all people are made. By no means least, it is the faith which we study to learn and teach so that by faith we might love God not only with all our heart, soul and bodily strength, but with all our mind as well.

Such a faith summons us to trust God's presence, promises, purposes and power to see us across Kierkegaard's 70,000 fathoms of meaninglessness and nihilism. It is not a faith which can be branded and packaged so as to neutralise the element of risk and the insecurities consequent upon venturing into what is for now unknown and unknowable. A Church which, in the words of Wesley Carr, purports "to know the unknowable, solve the insoluble and make reality go away" has subverted such faith and reduced it to mere religion. Such religious reductionism also results when a Church seeks to become itself the object of faith with its ceremonies and sacraments, dogmas and doctrines, rules and regulations functioning as surrogates for faith rather than as supply points and signposts to aid pilgrims on their way. The Church which will be most serviceable to faith is a Church which will be humble enough to exalt its second-order significance whether in the realms of belief, behaviour or what it means to belong to the People of God and the Body of Christ. This is the Church which will gladly accept that faith as trust is the gift for which it may well provide the packaging whilst resisting the religious temptation to itself become the brand.

Relics of Religion – Footprints of Faith

"There are various kitches: Catholic, Protestant, Jewish, Communist, Facist, democratic, feminist, European, American, national, international ... ... Movements rest not so much on rational attitudes as on the fantasies, images, words and archetypes that come together to make up this or that ... kitsch". (Milan Kundera: *The Unbearable Lightness of Being*).

Bearing the blood of Jesus around the streets of Bruges is not to be undertaken lightly. Indeed it weighed heavily, not only on account of the elaborately bejewelled casket in which the phial of blood was contained, but mostly because of my own bewilderment as to exactly what was going on here.

The Diocese of Lincoln has a long-standing ecumenical link with the Roman Catholic Diocese of Bruges, and it is usual for representatives from Lincoln to be graciously invited to share in the Procession of the Holy Blood, which is an ancient ritual taking place on Ascension Day each year. The procession is an impressive sequence of scenes from the Bible together with re-enactments of how the relic came to Bruges at the time of the Crusades and has been venerated ever since. The climax of the event is the bearing of the Holy Blood of Christ through the City in its weighty reliquary gleaming gold and studded with precious stones. It takes two to carry it for very short periods at a time.

Why my bewilderment? I am certain it has nothing to do with people being hoodwinked into believing in the authenticity of a relic which even the most senior clergy would not assert without a great deal of qualification. My sense is that few of those who line the route, fall to their knees and cross themselves as the relic passes before them, truly believe that this is the blood of Jesus taken and preserved by Joseph of Arimathea after washing the body of the crucified Christ. Neither do I find myself exercised by the various theological rationales offered for the cult of relics down through the centuries. It does make sense to honour the remains of those martyred for the sake of the Gospel and to treasure them as organs of the Holy Spirit. These were arguments put forward by Jerome and Augustine, and they should not be despised.

Still I remain uneasy. Perhaps it is because the justification offered by the Church Fathers might be sustainable in relation to relics of the saints and martyrs, but here was blood purporting to be of Christ Himself – and all sorts of theological complications loom over the horizon at that point! Yet the Church through the centuries has demonstrated remarkable agility in the performance of theological gymnastics when it comes to issues of this kind, so why should I feel unduly concerned about the Holy Blood of Bruges?

On further reflection, the answer seems to be more to do with the elaborate reliquary itself than with the relic it contains. Here is a classic example of the container somehow becoming more important than the contents – and the container speaks of hierarchical power and ecclesiastical authority. This has more to do with religion than faith. When the Church ostentatiously wraps up the treasure it purports to guard and share, we have good reason to suspect that these relics are relics of religion rather than symbols or signs of faith. The message being sent out to those who see the procession passing by in Bruges on Ascension Day – and in countless other places where such events take place year on year – is that not only does the Church possess the blood of the Saviour or the bones of the Saints, but it has the power to package, process and display them as and when it wills. So long as this cult of relics is driven by benign and benevolent motives, as I believe to be the case in Bruges, then it might be felt that this local expression of folk religion tinged with civic pride does little harm. Indeed, I felt deeply moved by the whole experience for reasons I will come to in a moment. But not far beneath the surface lingers a suspicion to do with the corrosive tendencies of religion when it comes to seizing upon the simple essentials of the Christian faith and co-opting them to serve agendas which have more to do with worldly power than spiritual enrichment. It will be recalled that the Second Council of Nicea in 787 AD anathematized those who despised holy relics and laid down that no Church should be consecrated without them. This vested ecclesiastical authorities with huge power as they determined the provenance and authenticity of relics which thereby came to condition rather than convey personal piety and faith. These relics of religion are redolent of something sinister which is in evidence when objects become objects of worship and God becomes either domesticated or, what is worse, recruited to sponsor and endorse essentially secular self-serving aspirations.

But nonetheless I was moved by the Bruges experience and it is time to explore why. Above all, I think it was to do with walking in the footsteps of faith. It was not so much the relic itself that mattered as the people who had carried it, looked upon it and treasured it for hundreds of years. It was not the relic which was the guarantor of their faith, but their faith which guaranteed the relic an aura of sanctity and a lasting place in our affections. This seems to be at the heart of a growing urge to go on pilgrimage, and so follow in the steps of those who have gone before us as followers of the Way. Surely for such pilgrims the authenticity of otherwise of an object or person or event linked to the place of pilgrimage is less important than being in via with those who have walked this way in the past and whose faith and hope inspires us still. "Faith gives substance to our hopes and convinces us of realities we do not see". So begins the great chronicle of faith which dominates the final chapters of the Letter to the Hebrews, and we in our turn are urged "to run with resolution the race which lies ahead of us" (Heb. 12 vs 1). Furthermore, we are to do so with "our eyes fixed on Jesus, the pioneer and perfecter of faith" (vs 2). Whilst our disciplines of contemplation and meditation can be immensely enriched by resting our eyes on icons, artworks, or even elaborate reliquaries, still we know that it is only when we journey in faith with our eyes fixed on Jesus that we progress on the road that leads to life, and life in all its fullness (John 10 vs 10). This being the case, it is hardly surprising that participation in the Procession of the Holy Blood made its mark on my memory and reached through my reservations regarding the relics of religion to lift my spirits as I walked in the footsteps of faith. These words of R. S. Thomas speak into both my dilemma and its resolution:

"Why no! I never thought other than
That God is the great absence
In our lives, the empty silence
Within the place where we go
Seeking, not in hope to
Arrive or find.
He keeps the interstices
In our knowledge, the darkness
Between the stars.
His are the echoes
We follow, the foot prints he has
Just left." (Collected Poems, Dent, London 1993 p. 220)

Of course, running through these reflections on where relics relate to the tension between faith and religion are a number of themes to do with the very nature of theological enquiry and the tools placed at the theologian's disposal. For example, we are reminded that theology can never be merely an exercise in religious archaeology whereby we seek to unearth and burnish what was believed, practised and prized in the past. Such discoveries enhance our understanding of what informed, inspired and motivated our predecessors on the pilgrimage of faith, but as soon as an article or artefact of faith becomes in itself an object of veneration rather than a way-mark for those whose eyes were fixed on Jesus, then it has become a relic of religion with all the attendant risks thereby entailed. Theology is about many new departures, but as yet no arrivals. It looks back only to see where others have been, but it is likely to itself be on the way to somewhere else. It will drink deeply from wells sunk by those who have travelled the way of faith, and it will heed the signposts, stumbling blocks and culs-de-sac that others have mapped for our guidance. It will guard the base-camp of received wisdom, but it will never allow such wisdom to become as it were a reliquary wherein unfathomable mysteries purport to be comprehensively contained. Rather it will see the base-camp as a new point of departure on the journey into God's truth – but with a constant eye on the footprints of those who may well have been that way before. Maybe Religious Studies or Sociology of Religion will be able to dwell without more ado on the relics of religion, but theology at its best will always be about following in the footsteps of faith – and leaving new ones for others to follow after.

There is also a lesson to be learned from my Bruges experience when it comes to determining exactly what it is that makes an argument a theological argument. Putting it bluntly, we are doing theology when, whatever or whoever the subject may be, the object is God. God can never be the subject of a theological sentence – in that sense God doesn't do theology. Rather, theology is a discipline undertaken by human beings who may well write sentences such as "God is the Creator of the world" where God functions grammatically as the subject of the sentence but, of course, the full sentence should read: "We believe that God is the Creator of the world". Our Creeds are very carefully formulated in this respect so that the subject of credal statements is the one declaring their faith, and God is the object of these as of all truly theological statements.

Deriving from the Greek words for "God (*theos*)" and "talk/meaning (*logos*)" the word "theology" can be translated as "God-talk" in the sense that it is us talking about God rather than God talking to us. The Bible appears to be full of examples of God talking and "thus says the Lord" occurs countless times. Likewise, people past and present talk of God speaking to them so that they will habitually say "the Lord called me" to do so and so or "led me" to a certain course of action. But once again we must underline that these statements are shorthand for "I believe the Lord spake thus or thus". We may well credit those who write or speak in such a way with an authority which causes us to describe them as inspired or revelatory. In such cases we believe that God is using such people to convey God's word and will through them to us and they may be hailed as Holy Scripture on account of their revelatory power. Yet the authority pertaining to such utterances differs in degree but not in kind from all utterances in which God may appear to be the subject i.e. the one speaking, but in fact the speaker or writer is in every case human with God as the object of what is said or written.

One of our difficulties is that the subject / object language we habitually use is confusing and ambiguous. For example, we tend to talk in terms of idolatry as God being reduced to a mere object. God the Creator (or Subject) has become a creature (or object). So when I say that for an argument to be a theological argument, whatever or whoever the subject may be, the object must be God, am I not committing idolatry? Only if we fail to see that the same kind of shorthand employed in such sentences as "thus says the Lord" is also at work here. What we are really saying when we say that a creature (object) cannot be worshipped because it is not God the Creator (subject), is that we (subject) believe that God the Creator (object) cannot have His status as object of worship usurped by anything or anyone He has made.

Now I can't help feeling that when it comes to the cult of relics

– the "relics of religion" as I have called them – we simply compound the confusion and ambiguity all too evident in our subject / object language in relation to God. At the very least by interposing an object between ourselves as subjects and God the ultimate object of our yearning and adoration we are making it more difficult to think of theology as talk about God i.e. with us as the subjects and God as the object of such talk. God who is the eternal, original and unique Subject who ensures that all that is in heaven and earth can ultimately only ever be objects of His creative will, may indeed will that objects of His creation serve as windows into His being and nature. After all, this is crucial to our understanding of sacraments and their place in God's economy of revelation and salvation. But we have learned to handle God's sacramental gifts with extreme reverence and great care. We do well to counsel caution when it comes to the proliferation of what the Church authorises as sacraments, and Protestants have been especially reluctant to recognise sacraments other than those which have the mark of dominical authority. We recognise the risks involved both in terms of the potential for sacramental faith to succumb to the seductions of superstition, and also that where there are many and varied acts or objects validated as having some kind of sacred or sacramental significance the likelihood of abuse by unscrupulous or unstable religious practitioners is inevitably increased. The relics of religion should carry a health warning because of their potential effect on faith in God who as ultimately the single Subject in relation to creation must remain the sole Object of our worship, study and service.

Incidentally, in the Churches of Florence are to be found many relics, from Eucharistic wine congealed into the Blood of Christ at S. Ambrogio to the fresco of the Annunciation in Santissima Annunziata believed to have been miraculously accomplished by angelic intervention. Yet for many people the most significant relic is the finger of Galileo preserved in the Museo di Storia della Scienza. It has been used as the title for an important book by

Peter Atkins who has consistently challenged religious belief in the light of modern science (*Galileo's Finger* . OUP 2003). It would appear that atheistic scientism has its own relics which might be the sincerest form of flattery or, alternatively, cause religious people who rely on relics to at least pause for thought. Perhaps the Florentines showed characteristic prudence when Orsanmichele, originally a grain store which became a Church when an image of the Virgin was credited with miraculous powers, continued to double up as a grain store!

Would the safest way be to dispense, as many do, with all icons, artworks or even sacraments themselves in order to secure ourselves against such risks? Not if we ensure a proper and balanced relationship between faith and religion. We have suggested that religion is inclined towards the recruitment of God to serve our human agendas, and there can be little doubt that sacramental elements and sacred objects have proved irresistible to those tempted to manipulate them to promote their own ends in relation to power or wealth or both. This is made especially easy when religious institutions, for whatever reason, identify such elements or objects so closely with God's presence, grace or power that they become virtually synonymous with God Himself, and so objects equate to God when it comes to the object of theological discourse and engagement.

Nevertheless, such sacramental elements and sacred objects have a vital role to play in the service of faith rather than religion. Religion wants to use them to condition, control and govern the faith of adherents. That is always likely to be the case when faith is colonised by the categories of religion. But if faith is about putting our agendas at the service of God then it is such faith which will ensure that elements and objects, events and exemplars of many kinds can inform and enrich our spiritual journey without allowing them to compromise the uniqueness of God who, when it comes to doing theology, whatever or whoever the subject may be, will always be the sole object of all we think and say and do.

When it comes to guaranteeing the truth and authenticity of the faith we profess, we need all the help we can get. Yet there are no short cuts. Grace is free, but it is not cheap. This is a lesson reinforced by the likes of Kierkegaard and Bonhoeffer, and it can never be repeated often enough. When organised Christianity is at its most bullish as an agent of religion it is generally to be found offering inducements of many kinds to those anxious to access the God brand without paying the price which costly discipleship demands. If, as Rowan Williams has reminded us, martyrdom was a key indicator of Christian identity in the early years it was not long before salvation in this world and the next was on offer at prices which enriched the Church but which required far less than martyrdom from willing subscribers. At the Reformation, there was a ready audience for those who championed faith rather than works in the economy of salvation because this sounded altogether less threatening to their personal possessions and lifestyles. More recently, the prospect of being nominally a member of the Church and a recipient of its benefits, but without being required to put oneself out too much in return, has characterised a great deal of western Christianity.

Whilst it is not difficult to see such dilutions of discipleship as clearly contrary to what Jesus required of His followers, still the temptation for the Church to collude with such distortions has often proved irresistible. When the Church offers eternal life on the easy plan with terms and conditions predicated more on success and prosperity than the bearing of a cross, then it is more likely to be about religion than faith. Likewise, and to underline how often opposite poles attract, organisations are more likely to be about religion than faith when they make inordinate demands on their members, which lead to acts of violence or destruction in the service of ends which are not so much faith-based as socio-political in their ideological provenance. In both cases the invoking of means and mechanisms managed and manipulated by the institutions themselves is characteristic of their *modus operandi* so that whether to lower or raise the requirements to be a member and a beneficiary is a function of a religious regime rather than a community of faith.

Whilst these extremes seem to take us a long way from the rather recondite world of relics and rituals, the crucial point is that faith has been placed at the mercy of institutionalised intermediaries which are more interested in securing their own secular prospects than in prospecting a less certain and more costly future in the footsteps of those "who won God's approval because of their faith" (Hebrews 11 vs 39).

So back to Bruges where the Bishop, Roger Vangheluwe, sums up in a prayer how the relics of religion might by God's grace lead us to follow in the footsteps of faith:

Lord Jesus Christ,
Speak to us in the language of images,
Let us see what your life was
And how you experienced the deepest core of our being.
Touch us, so that we become strong
in order to go on the pilgrimage of life,
in which You are our predecessor,
to-day and forever. AMEN.

Faith, Religion and Revelation

"An honest religious thinker is like a tightrope walker. He almost looks as though he were walking on nothing but air. His support is the slenderest imaginable. And yet it really is possible to walk on it". (Ludwig Wittgenstein).

"Revelation is a process not a printout". (Bishop David Jenkins)

In the previous chapter we touched on the nature of theology and the need to be clear that God is the sole object of theological discourse, whatever or whoever the subject matter may be. We saw dangers in interposing between God and people of faith any kinds of objects which may threaten the exclusive theological objectivity of God. Of course, words are objects in this sense with the potential to assume something like divine status in the realms of religion, and we noted that whereas human beings are always the grammatical subject in theological sentences, it has been assumed that some of these human talkers about God speak or write with an authority such that what they say can be credibly described as the word of the Lord. The words of Scripture comprising the Holy Bible have pride of place for Christians in this respect, and so we find ourselves challenged as to the nature of such revelatory texts and their precise relationship to God as the object of theological language. When such texts are elevated to a status virtually equivalent to God himself, then there is a real risk that those who claim authority to validate and interpret such texts take to themselves powers which can all too easily be recruited to serve agendas which may or may not belong to God – something we have identified as characteristic of religion and a threat to the integrity of faith. On the other hand, to deny to these texts any authority other than that conveyed by their intrinsic literary merits would be to deprive Christian faith of much that is essential to its distinctive content and inspirational character. Christopher Rowland summarises the situation very succinctly:

"The great divide in Christianity is between those who think that God requires of humanity submission to a book which has been given divine approval, and those who regard the Bible as a book whose authority has been given as a result of human use over centuries and which has been shown in different ways to be a text which is indispensable to the Christian religion. Does the Bible compel assent because of its intrinsic authority, therefore, or because of an authority bestowed on it by use and its effects?" (*Reading the Bible*. SCM 2007 p 31).

So we find ourselves asking whether Revelation in general and Scriptural Revelation in particular, belong more to the relics of religion than the footprints of faith.

***

Our current season of discontent across the Christian world in relation to Gay and Lesbian issues has brought the worst out of everyone in terms of theological coherence – or lack of it.

My mail has been peppered with urgings from all sides as to the nature of truth and the right way to view Revelation. What strikes me most of all, and saddens me greatly, is the theological aridity of much of this. The so-called traditionalist arguments seem shallow and ill considered, and I am constantly reminded of people who spend their lives giving good advice to those who are happier than they are! So much of it is cold and calculating in its desire to do harm and cause hurt, and whilst much of this can be put down to gratuitous homophobia, there is also evidence of theological illiteracy in relation to Revelation in general, and scriptural revelation in particular. It is not difficult to sympathise with Carter Hayward's commitment to *"Saving Jesus From Those Who Are Right"* (Augsburg Fortress 1999).

On the other hand, those arguing from what is usually

thought of as a liberal perspective often display a lamentable poverty of spirit and imagination when it comes to weighing whether and how God's will in relation to such matters has been revealed in the past and can still be known by us today.

That is why it is worth while to look again at the concept of Revelation and in particular at the contribution made by liberal theology to what is sometimes a divisive and contentious issue for Christians. This is not intended to be a comprehensive theological overview, but a gentle journey into well-charted but nonetheless still fascinating territory. Amongst more recent contributions see, on the one hand, *Scripture and the Authority of God* by N. T. Wright (SPCK 2005) and on the other, *What the Bible Really Teaches* by Keith Ward (SPCK 2004). This subject clearly highlights tensions between those labelled liberal and conservative but I am convinced that this tension is a necessary one if we are going to do justice to the temperamental diversity prevalent amongst Christian believers journeying together in search of God and God's will.

For example, I once found myself in a protracted correspondence with a Priest who was proud to describe himself as a conservative evangelical. From his congregation had emerged a candidate for Ordination, and as he was pursuing Non-Stipendiary Ministry he would be required to train on the Regional Course for which I had some responsibility. This caused the Priest a great deal of anxiety because he doubted the soundness of my theology, and was sure that his carefully nurtured candidate would be corrupted by my liberal tendencies. In the course of our correspondence I conjured with the image of fellow-travellers on a journey of discovery, and ran past him the idea that some are by temperament keepers of the base camp, whilst others incline towards exploring the frontiers and pressing on into the unknown. Perhaps this describes conservatives and liberals respectively.

As we have seen, conservatives keep the base-camp of

received tradition with that authority which comes with the wisdom of the ages, and truths tested by time and experience. On the other hand, liberals are those who are temperamentally disinclined to settle in a place in order to guard and protect it from philosophical predators or mischievous marauders. They go in pursuit of the truth wherever it might lead and if that results in exposure to risk when it comes to challenging received orthodoxies then that may be a price worth paying for the prize of intellectual integrity. The truth is greater than we can currently know and so the spirit of theological adventure must be given the chance to flourish.

Sadly, although I think I managed to convince my correspondent that I was sincere in my sense of need for him and conservatives like him to guard the base-camp from which I and other liberals could venture on our theological explorations, I did not get anywhere near convincing him that he needed me. Guarding the treasure of Tradition was all that mattered as far as he was concerned, and that was an end in itself. He was prepared to concede no sense of thereby making it possible for those of a different temperament to press on into the unknown because, as far as he was concerned, what there is to know has been made known through the inspired text of Scripture and there are no further epistemological frontiers to be explored.

This encounter goes to the heart of the debate about Revelation, because it underlines how important it is for conservatives and liberals to stay in touch with each other on this issue. It will not do for conservatives to caricature liberals as "those who have no understanding of Revelation" as one fellow-Bishop told me in an attempt to be helpful. But neither will it do for liberals to imply that Reason has effectively discredited Revelation and has taken over its privileged position in the hierarchy of theological authorities - thereby destroying the base-camp which resources the liberal quest and instigates our questions.

In an article in the Church of England Newspaper (26th June 2003), Michael Marshall reminded us of how C. S. Lewis, in his book *Mere Christianity* speaks of "deep Church". This is in order to try and breach the artificial dichotomy between "high" and "low" Church which to some extent reflects the chasm which has opened up between conservative and liberal theologians. "What he meant" says Marshall, "was that the Church throughout its history has needed, and indeed still needs, to get beneath the surface and the superficial meaning implied in the medium of its doctrines, and quarry out the essential message of Christ." Marshall goes on to show how such a "deep Church" might handle current issues in ethics and personal morality with, of course, a particular eye to the Jeffrey John affair. It was a brave piece in a very conservative newspaper, and I was intrigued to see that it ended in mid-sentence with the conclusion omitted (that's enough liberalism. Ed!).

But Marshall was simply capturing something of Rowan Williams' address at the first daily Eucharist at the 1998 Lambeth Conference. He preached on the parable of the men building their houses on rock and sand respectively. In Matthew's Gospel the wise man builds on the firm foundation of rock ready-made for the purpose, whilst in Luke's Gospel the man digs deep to find the rock on which to build. The Archbishop reminded the Conference of how we needed to both build on the foundation which is Christ, and yet also dig deep to discover that on which we can reliably build today.

This tension between Revelation as given for our unqualified acceptance and Revelation as something to be quarried from the deposit of faith, something for which we must continue to dig deep, is vital to the integrity of a Church which aspires to build wisely and not prove foolish.

As their contribution towards a holistic understanding of Revelation, liberals will be issuing a consistent reminder that like cheques which must be cashed by the payee, so Revelation must be "cashed" by people whose personal experience and rationality exist as essential to their receptivity. The Magi needed a star as well as a text to guide them, and this encourages us in our belief that God's revelatory purpose is scriptural but more than scriptural – it takes seriously the potential for reason and experience to enhance "people's awareness of God showing them things" (Helen Oppenheimer: *Making Good*. SCM 2001 p. 91).

However, liberals must resist the temptation to privilege Reason and Experience to such an extent that no transcendent communication is allowed for in the economy of Revelation. As Michael Langford has put it,

"for historical religions such as Christianity, *some* religious assertions need to be made if one is to have a faithful continuation of the tradition ... ... The traditional Christian, including the traditional liberal Christian, believes that behind and beyond the physical universe there is a loving creator who is reaching down (sic) to us in love, and that this would be true even if no person realised it and no religious grammar presently recognised it. Behind all human constructions, there is a discovery, a truth waiting to be revealed". (*A Liberal Theology for the Twenty-First Century*. Ashgate Press 2001 pp. 130-1).

There is a certain irony in the fact that political and economic liberals are strident in their challenge to those who chart the history of e.g. America or Australia from the date when the colonists arrived. But theological liberals can tend towards a kind of modernist imperialism when they speak as though God's truth had no reality before they found it out. To discover the truth about God is to light upon it and be enlightened by it – we do not invent it.

In relation to the specific debate about human sexuality, the tendency for both "sides" to over-reach themselves is all too apparent. Over time I have almost become allergic to sentences in letters on this subject which begin: "the plain meaning of scripture is ... ...". Keith Ward puts the matter well when he says

"Revelations are not, despite what some people might hope for, clear and precise sets of doctrines and commands. Taken at their deepest level, revelations are tremendously mysterious, and they are revelations of a being who remains ultimately mysterious. All genuine revelations are revelations of mystery ... ... they do not give definite and unambiguous answers to our direct questions."

He concludes with a typically pugnacious flourish: "Revelation, it is very clear, must be very unclear, if so much genuine and conscientious diversity can exist among those who seek to adhere to it" (*God – A guide for the Perplexed*. Oneworld Publications 2002 pp. 238-9).

Yet so many conservative commentators persist in asserting the unquestionable certainty of scriptural texts as though hermeneutics equate to some kind of wasting disease to be avoided at all costs. It is as if the recent centuries of biblical scholarship count for nothing as verses are plucked from their context and paraded as slogans, to which the faithful must rally or risk expulsion from the fold – an all too familiar religious tendency. Liberals feel compelled to challenge this uncritical use of scripture because they love the Bible, and have devoted to it too much of their powers of heart and mind to simply sit back and tolerate this abuse of God's gracious gift. There are good reasons to feel saddened by the worst excesses of such obscurantism because those of us whose spirituality and discipleship have been so enriched by the fruits of biblical scholarship, simply possess an evangelical zeal to help others experience these insights for themselves. At the beginning of the 20th Century Bishop John Percival lamented that "Whenever I hear devout and good men (sic) inveighing against the Higher Criticism, I have to confess that I listen with regret". (*Twenty Four Anglican Charges*) and at the beginning of the 21st Century we feel just as sad.

More than that, we might be forgiven for feeling angry when the lives and livelihoods of sometimes vulnerable people are put at risk by an appeal to scriptural authority which is cynically selective, historically naïve and verging on intellectual dishonesty. Strong words these may be, but they are as nothing compared to the vitriol to which many liberals have been subjected in recent times, and if we are wise to avoid meeting abuse with abuse, there is a place for righteous indignation to be expressed when the Bible we love is being abused, and people we love are thereby victimised.

As we face the challenges currently before us, we must hope and pray that those of a conservative temperament will recover their role as guardians of the base-camp, who protect the tradition against ill-informed and unsubstantiated critique, whilst encouraging others to pursue their God-given instincts for creative questioning and intellectual curiosity in the face of profound mysteries. My vision for mutuality and interdependence between liberals and conservatives depends upon such a recovery of role, and a revival of confidence amongst those traditionalists whose fearful defensiveness has been so detrimental to the cause of effective dialogue and perhaps owes more to religious zeal than trust-like faith.

But liberals have to put their house in order as well if such dialogue is to be fruitful. After all, it is not unknown for liberals to be selective in their use of biblical texts, and sometimes the degree of interpretation and contextualisation required owes more to prejudice than objectivity. Kierkegäard once cuttingly observed that if the Bible contained texts insisting that all Christians should be in receipt of a handsome pension by virtue of their faith, then no-one would be arguing for "interpretation" – that's readily understandable, we would say, and we have no need of scholars and professors to tell us what it really means. But because the Bible requires that we give what we have to the poor and take up our cross, then we seem to need any number of scholars and professors to interpret this obscure requirement, and to tell us that it probably doesn't mean what it appears to mean, and if it does, it doesn't apply to us. How often have we enlisted the tools of biblical criticism, not in the cause of clarification and a genuine search for the truth, but in order to bolster a view we have adopted on other grounds? Frankly, some of my liberal correspondents in the gay and lesbian debate have been very ingenious but often disingenuous in their appeal to certain principles of interpretation when dealing with uncomfortable texts. Again, this owes more to religion and its susceptibility to recruitment by proprietorial agendas than it does to a free and fearless faith.

It is salutary to be reminded that in his *Principles of Philosophy*, René Descartes wrote this:

"But above all else we must impress on our memory the overriding rule that whatever God has revealed to us must be accepted as more certain than anything else. And although the light of reason may, with the utmost clarity and evidence, appear to suggest something different, we must still put our entire faith in divine authority rather than in our own judgement."

So what is the way forward?

Clearly the fundamental issue at stake in the present crisis threatening the unity of our Church is the issue of biblical authority which, in its turn, is but one element in a wider debate about the nature of Revelation. Whilst human sexuality has dominated the horizon, it is only a presented issue. The real fault lines feature in relation to how God's word can be revelatory in the 21st Century, and how God's will can be known in this generation. David Brown has effectively shown how holy texts are always being re-read so that there is no pristine meaning that can be isolated from the constant process of reassimilation. Tradition is imagining afresh what a text says, not simply relaying it from age to age. (*Tradition and Imagination*. OUP 1999 and reviewed by Rowan Williams in *Theology* 2000, p 452). But this assumes that there is a revelatory deposit, something given, which is subject to imaginative reassimilation. Reading scripture is a process of discovery not invention, and what is discovered as if for the first time, is what God has revealed as God's word for all time. Affirming the giveness of the text, and the need to guard it against hostile predators, must remain as a vital task for those Christians whose gifts and instincts can most effectively serve the cause of conservation. But conservation cannot in itself do justice to the dynamics of Revelation which require gifts of creative imagination and interpretative flair if past events, and the words used to relay those events, are to become good news to the ears of our contemporaries and those who come after us. Liberals see Revelation as progressive, and David Jenkins speaks for many when he says that

"the claim that the stamp of revelation authorizes one to ignore either history or science only guarantees that any form of belief in God will appear to the wider world to be an outmoded superstition ... ... We are not called to be faithful ostriches burying our heads in the deposits of the religious past. The sacred formulations of past believers are rich resources to be read in the light of our present reality – both historical and scientific – as we present believers strive to live and expound faith in God today". (*The Calling of a Cuckoo*. Continuum 2003 p. 80).

Seeing the Bible not as a source book but rather as a resource on our journey into the mystery of God, is one of he key contributions liberals can make to an understanding of Revelation which is not static but dynamic, not monochrome but pluriform, not dead but living, not merely true as a matter of fact but true as a matter of faith and experience. This is the kind of faith Christ calls us to share. It is a faith which is forever opening up new fronts and frontiers to be explored, as well as offering the security of a base-camp firmly established on the foundations of biblical texts, traditional interpretations of those texts – and the conviction that the Bible is a site of many meanings yet to be made manifest. To espouse such a faith demands of us that we make common cause as liberals and conservatives, because we need each other if Revelation is not to be reduced to pre-modern obscurantism on the one hand, or post-modern relativism on the other. If there was less conservative religion and liberal religion in the world, and rather more conservative faith and liberal faith, we might come to learn from each other just how truly revealing Revelation can be.

Vicarious Faith or Religion-Lite?

"Anglicans are people who go around being nice to people and hoping they will guess the reason why".
"We go to Church for the sake of God who is present – and the people who aren't".

For several decades Dot Cotton of *Eastenders* has cornered the market in, well, dotty soap characters who go to Church and pepper their folksy moralising with biblical texts citing both chapter and verse. Even when she became Dot Branning on her marriage to Jim, who definitely did not do God, still her convictions remained firm. That is until she is mugged on her own doorstep when about the Lord's business. This causes her to abandon her Christian beliefs and it was the intention of the script editors that she would now foreswear faith and get a life. In the event, no sooner had the story-line got underway than the producers were inundated with letters of protest demanding that Dot should not be allowed to lose her faith, and the protest was so strong that a nifty change in the plot was needed so that in pretty short order Dot recovers her Christian convictions, returns to Church and resumes her role as Albert Square's resident God botherer.

What lay behind these protests? It was clearly not an orchestrated campaign by a religious lobby fearful that yet another relic of Christian culture was about to disappear. Most of the letters and e-mails came from people who seemed to have little or no affiliation to organised religion, and were generally not Churchgoers. It would appear that whilst they themselves did not give outward expression to Christian belief, they were glad that Dot did so and, what is more significant, they felt that in some sense she did so on their behalf so that if she lost her faith they would be losers as well.

This provides an intriguing insight into the phenomenon of vicarious faith which continues to flourish in ways that tend to confound those who espouse without question theories of secularisation. It is a phenomenon with which Churches, and especially the Church of England, are very familiar. It was explored some years ago in the symposium *Say One for Me* edited by Wesley Carr (SPCK 1992) and more recently in *Praying for England* Eds. Samuel Wells and Sarah Coakley (Continuum 2008). It manifests itself whenever people who do not overtly profess or practice the Christian faith are glad and grateful that there are those who do so for them.

When I first became a Vicar of a Parish, I went to the Church every day at 8 a.m., tolled the bell, and said Morning Prayer. No one ever joined me and during a particularly cold spell I was persuaded that I could just as easily say the Office in the comfort of my study. So I stopped journeying to the Church and tolling the bell. It was not long before I began to have my ear bent by people who first of all joked about how they always knew when it was time to leave for work, or the bus was late, because they heard the Church bell ringing. But I quickly realised that they were trying to say something far more serious to me about how glad and grateful they were that I was known to be there, at the heart of their community, praying for them even if they could not or would not pray for themselves. I went back to saying Morning Prayer in Church, and tolling the bell, as Canon Law wisely requires!

We go to Church for the sake of the God who is present and the people who aren't. That we are in Church to worship God is presumably beyond question, but we pay little regard to this vicarious role whereby we represent a community to God and God to a community in ways which may be implicit rather than explicit, but are nevertheless significant. There is a genuine sense in which when we are at worship and prayer we are surrounded not only by that great cloud of witnesses who have gone before us (see Hebrews chapter 12 verse 1, as Dot would be quick to remind us), but also by family members, neighbours and acquaintances who we bring with us and who are glad we are there for them.

Sometimes we are taken by surprise when, especially in rural villages, large numbers of people are aroused to protest when it is rumoured the Parish Church might close, even if the majority of those protesting seldom if ever darken its doors. But it is part of the same phenomenon, with at least some sense that not only the Church building, but also the prayer and worship expressive of its on-going life, is for the good of the whole community which would be impoverished without it. Unsurprisingly, the greatly reduced sense of community characteristic of urban and suburban contexts means that such protests in relation to the closure of Churches is far more muted – and my hunch is that for this very reason the protests about Dot's loss of faith are far more likely to have come from those places where the only plausible person available to purvey a vicarious faith is a fictional character in a TV Soap.

Not unrelated to this notion of vicarious faith is the idea that a Christian presence and ministry should be on offer always and everywhere, with few if any conditions requiring to be met in order to access them. In addition to maintaining a building and ensuring a cohort of Christians committed to worshipping and praying for and on behalf of the community, it will also involve making available the Occasional Offices, pastoral care, seasonal celebrations, opportunities for corporate fellowship and prophetic witness to and for the community as and when required. It will usually entail the presence of an appropriately trained and authorised minister who the wider community will significantly call "Vicar" whatever alternative titles the institutional Church may use to designate them. There will be an expectation that Baptisms, Weddings and Funerals will be provided as of right to local people, perhaps in return for a modest fee, and with no significant hurdles to be cleared in terms of past, present or future profession or practice of the Christian faith. The Church will function to all intents and purposes as a public utility from which citizens are entitled to receive a service without more ado.

Whilst to some extent these expectations relate to all mainstream Churches, they fall mostly upon the Church of England as the Established Church, with a parochial system predicated on the tacit assumption that all are to be counted in unless by choice or default they count themselves out. Indeed, Archbishop George Carey once commented on how the Church of England agreed to his non-churchgoing parents' request for him to be Baptised. "The Church of England included me", he said, "before I included myself". The same can be said of the other services provided by a Parish Church for the community within which it is set, and it comes very close to the notion of vicarious faith whereby the Church and its members choose to include those who may not as yet have included themselves. If people don't go to Church, the Church they don't go to is the Church of England.

All statistics and indicators of attitudes to religious observance suggest that there continues to be a decline in the numbers of those choosing to access these services, even when they are made available on the basis of vicarious faith rather than requiring evidence of personal commitment and conviction. Yet the percentage of the population participating in seasonal celebrations requesting the Occasional Offices and visiting Churches and Cathedrals for more than merely heritage reasons remains remarkably high, and so long as the Church is able and willing to be there for people in such ways there will continue to be a significant demand to be met. Furthermore, in addition to these traditional patterns of ministry and pastoral provision we need to note the proliferation of Chaplaincy services in a wide range of social and institutional settings. Indeed, it is possible that more people will come into contact with a minister of religion through Chaplaincy than through encountering the "Vicar" in the place where they live. The ministry of a Chaplain is another expression of vicarious faith insofar as the Chaplain indwells a hospital or a prison or a school as a faith commitment on behalf of all those for whom that is their temporary home or place of work.

Now we could wax eloquent about all of this, and parade stories and statistics which would seem to powerfully contradict the doom-laden predictions of decline and extinction which characterise much that passes for comment on religious affairs in most of the media. But before we do, we must sound a note of caution which relates directly to the theme we have been exploring. Because we need to ask ourselves whether we are not so much in the business of celebrating vicarious faith as colluding with religion–lite. We referred in the Introduction to how the Church of England has acquired a reputation for having discovered "just exactly how much religion the average Englishman (sic) can stand", and we saw this as something of a virtue insofar as it leaves space for faith to flourish unconstrained by over-fussy ecclesiastical requirements. Yet we are left to wonder whether we have in fact freed up faith to flourish in the fresh air of liberality, or simply watered down the reasonable requirements for religious identity and affiliation in the interests of maintaining our market share and the popular vote.

This is a crucial question because it goes to the heart of many debates in local Churches about how we relate to those who want the Church to be there for them but show little inclination towards regular commitment. It also challenges many Clergy who devote a great deal of time and energy to meeting demands from such people with little likelihood of a return in terms of enhanced participation in Church life – and members of the congregation resent Clergy time thus diverted from what they believe to be their needs and entitlements. If we conclude that all we are offering in such ministry is religion-lite then I would have to sympathise entirely with such frustrations. We have seen that whether religion is lite or full-bodied it can never be an end in itself but must always be at the service of faith and its nurture. It may allow people to have a little bit of God in their lives, just as they might like to wear a piece of religious jewellery, but it does nothing to foster faith in God and the living of a Christ-centred life. If there is too much religion in the world and not enough faith, then colluding with requests for yet more religion, however lite, must run plain counter to what Christian ministry and mission is ultimately all about.

So can we sustain a case for the Church continuing to offer ministry on the terms with which we have become familiar, but which are now subject to more critical scrutiny than ever before? If we are clear as to what we mean by "vicarious faith", and how it relates to our overall apprehension of the Christian Gospel at work in Church and Society, then I am sure we can answer this question positively and in a generous spirit.

First of all, we need to acknowledge that vicariousness goes to the heart of what Jesus was about in His life as well as death. Unfortunately, this aspect of Jesus' person and purpose has been hi-jacked by an almost exclusive emphasis on His death and the penal substitutionary theory of atonement. As a result, those who quite reasonably raise concerns about how someone can bear guilt on behalf of someone else and, although innocent themselves, meet the requirements of a penal justice system by undergoing the consequential punishment in the place of the guilty party, remain suspicious of the whole notion of vicariousness which is rendered guilty by association with a doctrine deemed dubious and morally suspect. However, there is a dimension to vicariousness which is more to do with solidarity than substitution. Referring to the key text, II Corinthians 5 vss 14 – 15, David Catchpole asserts that "the preposition 'for' (*uper*) is the solidarity preposition – nothing to do with substitution! It works by way of identification – incorporation, and is the counterpart of in (*en* as in 'in Christ')". (Notes to lecture: *Jesus People, Easter People and the People of God.* 2007). Once we move from substitution to solidarity in our understanding of vicariousness we begin to see clearly how "vicarious faith" works on the basis of who Jesus was and what He came to achieve.

Although it is commonplace in some circles to talk about "inviting Jesus into your life", it is more appropriate to turn the invitation around the other way because, in fact, it is Jesus who invites us into His life. The essence of the Incarnation is that Jesus has entered into solidarity with humankind in ways which may be ontologically mysterious but which are existentially compelling. As our brother, He has entered fully into our humanity – He needs no invitation into our lives because He is already in intimate solidarity with us. But it is a solidarity which is not invasive or imposed. Rather, it invites us to respond in the same way as a guest responds to an invitation with a clear sense that what is being accepted or rejected is a gift which is simply waiting to be claimed. It is rather like the gift which we are told simply awaits our collection in the latest Reader's Digest draw – but in relation to God's grace the gift is real, really worth having and waiting to be claimed by everyone and not just the lucky few!

Jesus lived and died vicariously, and faith in Jesus can be likewise vicarious insofar as it is about that same overflowing of God's grace and goodwill in solidarity with those around us. Our faith is not vicarious in the sense that we believe and trust so that others don't have to. As with the assertion that Jesus died "for us", so the concept of vicarious faith is an oxymoron unless it is about solidarity rather than substitution. But if our faith overflows with God's grace and goodwill towards others then vicarious faith as a function of solidarity with those who may not yet have accepted Jesus' invitation into His life goes to the heart of our purpose as the People of God and the Body of Christ. When others presume upon our faith as giving some kind of expression to inchoate instincts and longings deep in their own minds and hearts, then such vicarious faith can be the calling card whereby God's invitation into the life of Christ is conveyed and communicated.

We have argued that whereas religion is too often about the recruitment of God to serve our agendas, faith is about putting our agendas at the service of God. This is never more so than when we gladly put our personal faith, and the faith of the Church as expressed through worship, prayer and pastoral care, at the service of those who no less than us are made in God's image and with us are numbered amongst those for whom Christ lived and died. By so doing, we are putting our faith at the disposal of God who, as Peter came to realise, "has no favourites" (Acts 10 vs 34). If religion inclines towards rigour and regulation when it comes to terms and conditions of membership, then it tends towards limiting the breadth of God's embrace. It may offer religion-lite to the ecclesiastical equivalent of an armchair football fan, but it falls well short of inspiring and nurturing faith in God's forgiveness and acceptance which Peter proclaimed for "everyone who trusts in Him" (Acts 10 vs 43). When Churchpeople grumble about those whose nominal Christianity seems to be parasitic on the faith and sacrificial commitment of regular paid-up members, perhaps they are behaving too much like religious adherents lamenting the prevalence of religion-lite. In so doing, they are placing limits of their own on what it means to belong to God and that "wideness of God's mercy", of which the hymn writer F. W. Faber wrote so eloquently, has been squeezed to accommodate a less expansive economy of grace.

However, when the Church and Church people positively welcome requests to "say one for me", and gladly make provision for those who want the baby "done", or a Church wedding because they retain some vestigial sense that it's the right thing to do, or a Christian funeral service when the undertaker and others offer alternatives, then the garment of faith is seen to have a generous hem and the prodigal impartiality of God is shown and shared.

So vicarious faith says something not only about the Incarnation and our belief that Jesus is there for us and for others in a spirit of solidarity and self-giving service, but also speaks of God the Father whose love is wide enough and deep enough to embrace all who are in need of a parent's care. Yet there is more, because vicarious faith also says something about how God the Holy Spirit is at work in the world.

For many people, and perhaps especially for those of a rigorously religious disposition, the Holy Spirit is experienced as violently invasive and extravagantly dramatic in its effects. Taking Acts 2 as the definitive paradigm for how the Spirit takes over the bodies and minds of faithful people, very obvious and public charismatic gifting is adopted as the key criterion whereby sound Christian identity can be recognised and confirmed. This is commonly characteristic of "born-again" Christianity, and for all that it manifests itself in apparently liberated and liberating expressions of praise and prayer, it tends to be contained within religious regimes where clear boundaries and strict discipline are much in evidence. It is as though this violent, invasive Spirit must be brought under control so that just as in some quarters sacramental grace comes to depend for its effectiveness upon the imprimatur of ecclesiastical authority, so the freedom and power of the Spirit needs to be harnessed and authenticated by those in positions of leadership and control.

On the other hand, it is possible to think of the Spirit as being more about indwelling than invasion. It is significant that what we call "Spirituality" is more likely to be couched in terms of contemplation, meditation, reflection and retreat than in terms of extravagant extroversion or hyperactivity. Here it is not so much the Spirit driving Jesus into the wilderness or coming upon the disciples as a rushing mighty wind which is to the fore. It is that power through the Spirit which grants inward strength and enables us "with deep roots and firm foundations ... to grasp what is the breadth and length and height and depth of Christ's love and to .. be filled with the very fullness of God" (Ephesians 3 vss 16 – 19). This indwelling Spirit is the very essence of faith in our Christ-like God whose "fullness" cannot possibly be contained by the restrictions of organised religion, but which can be trusted by faith to enrich our understanding, enlighten our path and bring us home. It is by the power of this indwelling Spirit that local Christians and congregations, Ministers and Chaplains, indwell the communities where they are called to live, work, worship and witness. It is a Spirit that requires to be released rather than regulated. It requires the wind of faith in order to blow where it wills, rather than religious stabilizers to determine its direction and destination. When we restrict access to that grace which is ours by faith, we may well do so in order to protect the purity and integrity of our religious convictions. But my hunch is that the Spirit of God can take care of herself, and when we take the risk of allowing our faith to be put at the disposal of others, such vicariousness has something of God about it and it will not return to us empty. All are in equal need of God's grace, and God's grace is equal to the needs of all.

It is now generally acknowledged that when people find faith for themselves it is usually under the influence of one other person over quite a long period of time. This suggests that faith experienced vicariously really does have the potential to win disciples for Christ, but only if we ourselves are convinced that this is possible as we take with us into our prayers and worship those who are glad we are saying one for them, glad that we will include them before they feel able to include themselves, and grateful that our ministry of concern and care is not conditioned by the quality of their religious commitment. Those who protested at Dot Cotton's loss of faith may have been indulging in some form of religion-lite, but they may well have been touched more than we know by her faith experienced vicariously and I, for one, am prepared to give them the benefit of the doubt.

Ministers of Religion: People of Faith

"On my notes on admission to hospital, by the side of the heading 'Spiritual' were the words: 'has a friend who is a Vicar'". (Heather M. Marshall *Safe in the Shadow*).

As far as the taxman is concerned, Clergy are Ministers of Religion. It is not a title Clergy would usually use to describe themselves or their colleagues other than on official documentation. Perhaps this indicates some reserve about being too closely identified with religion when it comes to how Clergy are described. However, it is more likely to indicate some distancing from the terminology employed by secular bureaucracy, and that would be entirely understandable.

However, the term "ministers of religion" does become of interest when we note that those to whom they minister are described as "the faithful". Presumably ministers of religion are not assumed to be unfaithful, but when religion and faith are subtly distinguished in such a way it offers another variation on the theme we are exploring. When lay people are described as faithful, and ministers are "of religion" this may simply offer a further example of how "faith" and "religion" are used interchangeably. On the other hand, we may be capturing echoes of a distinction being made between officially recognised representatives of Christianity who are thereby "religious" and those whose Christianity is the faith of a lay discipleship.

When some members of the Church are specially called, trained, Ordained and deployed to fulfil certain roles to which are attached titles, privileges and possibly some payment, then it is quite natural for them to be seen as set apart for the advancement of religion whilst others are simply required to be faithful. It is then a short step to suggesting that ministers of religion have a personal and proprietorial interest in the survival of organised Christianity and the institutional Church, whilst lay people hold to a faith uncomplicated by such religious concerns. Whilst the official representatives of religion are theoretically and theologically seen as set apart precisely to encourage and uphold the faith of the laity, the dynamics of religion can all too easily result in an overvaluing of the institution and its professional personnel, i.e. too much religion, and the belittling of day to day discipleship i.e. too little faith. This is not to say that the Gospel of Christ and the Kingdom of God does not require ministers of religion to advance their cause. There is no doubt in my mind that vocation, formation, Ordination and authorisation to Accredited ministries are gifts of God and means of grace. Yet as I have sought to demonstrate in other contexts, what in popular parlance and imagination is defined in terms of religion must always be at the service of faith – so that ministers of religion must first of all be themselves people of faith, called and sent to serve people of faith, lest a professional caste of Christians come to stand for Christianity as a whole and religious officialdom stifle rather than stimulate faithful witness.

So we welcome a marked emphasis in recent years on recognising and developing the gifts of lay people in our Churches. This has proved to be something of a growth industry with significant resources of money, people and enterprise being directed towards courses in lay ministry and discipleship. But it has not been without its critics.

First of all, there has been some fear that all this investment has been more to do with ministry than discipleship. Whilst the Tiller Report of 1983 (*A Strategy for the Church's Ministry* , John Tiller, CIO Publishing) and that other key manifesto *All are Called* (Church House Publishing 1985) captured the imagination and led to a sea-change in the way the contribution of lay people to parish ministry was perceived and valued, another report entitled *Called to be Adult Disciples* (GS 794 1987) barely registered on the radar. In more recent times those Adult Education Advisers dedicated to supporting and equipping lay people in their Monday to Saturday discipleship have typically lost out to the providers of ministry training when Diocesan budgets have been squeezed.

A second and related concern is to do with what has become known as the "clericalisation" of the laity. This entails identifying and training lay people to undertake tasks in liturgy, administration and pastoral care which have usually been seen as jobs for the Clergy. The extraordinary increase in the number of Readers relative to a declining cohort of Clergy has ensured that ministering God's Word in worship may fall as much to lay people as to those who are Ordained. Readers also exercise a valuable pastoral ministry and in both this and the leading of worship they are joined by members of Lay Ministry Teams. The result is that in a Diocese like Lincoln there are as many people holding the Bishop's Licence today as there were just before the First World War which was the high point of Beneficed Clergy presence in the 665 Parishes. Of course, now the majority of such Licensed Ministers are lay and in receipt of no remuneration. Yet they are present and active in their communities as Clergy were a century ago, so that they are sometimes seen as clerical clones where faithful lay witness has come to look more like the performance of religious duties.

Both these concerns are worth taking seriously although the first of them may be felt to assume too great a distinction between ministry and discipleship, and the second fails to acknowledge the extent to which lay involvement in leading worship and pastoral care, especially as vested in the Office of Churchwarden, has been a feature of Parish life for many centuries. Indeed, we might more effectively avoid the pitfalls of clericalization by seeing lay ministry as a development of the historic role of the Churchwarden rather than as delegation from the traditional role of the Clergy. However, the point remains that inherited structures of religious organisation can become totems to be preserved at all costs, and insofar as lay people are being used to prop up organised religion at the expense of a more freed up expression of faith, then the tail may well be wagging the dog.

A further, and again not unrelated concern, is that the distinctive contribution which faithful lay people can make to God's mission and ministry might be disabled by our religiously regulated courses of training and accreditation. I painfully recall the occasion when, at the end of a lay training course I led in a group of small rural Parishes in south Devon, one of the Churchwardens rose to offer a vote of thanks. He expressed gratitude for the trouble I had taken in travelling all that way on cold winter evenings to lead the course, and he pointed to the fact that numbers had steadily increased from one session to the next as evidence that it had all been a great success. But, he concluded, as a result of what he had learned on the course he would never be able to visit anyone in hospital again! What he meant was that he had visited people quite spontaneously and as a natural expression of his Christian faith and concern for others in their time of need. However, he would now be thinking too much about the do's and don'ts of visiting so that his instinctive bedside manner would be disabled by my checklist nagging away at the back of his mind. Of course, I immediately went away to work on my clearly deficient adult education techniques, but the underlying point about disabling faith-filled flair by demanding that everything be done right – something to which I fear religion is pathologically prone – remained to be addressed.

All this suggests that if ministers of religion are to be first of all people of faith, then God's faithful people must above all be guarded against the seductions of religious conformity if they are to contribute to the flourishing of Christianity in the 21st Century. And contribute they must. This is not just because financial constraints, or a shortfall in those offering for Ordained ministry, create a crisis which only the training and deployment of lay people can rectify. It is because a Church where God's calling and gifting of all faithful people is honoured is the Church which the New Testament teaches us to celebrate and replicate in the terms of our own context and times. It may be cynical to suggest that the Church of England only does what is right when it can no longer afford to do what is wrong, but if it is financial constraints which have driven the present trend towards realising the potential of lay people in ways which have not been typical in recent times, then so be it.

From the point of view of the Clergy, and especially Stipendiary Clergy in Parishes, this evolving scenario can be somewhat threatening. Although, as Anthony Russell and others have ably demonstrated (Anthony Russell: *The Clerical Profession* SPCK 1980), the role of the Parish Priest has undergone a good deal of evolution over the centuries, with the development of a clerical profession and the changing face of Incumbency being notable developments in recent times, still the role has been relatively secure and even the oldest dogs have not been required to learn too many new tricks.

However, over the last 30 years or so the pace of change has accelerated markedly as the Churches renegotiate their relationship with their cultural contexts, adjust to new social realities and find ways to manage their resources more efficiently and to greater effect. A number of time-honoured assumptions have been challenged, with rival approaches to theology, morality, social responsibility and ecclesiology seeking to influence the formulation of programmes and priorities. *The Ordained Ministry: Numbers, Cost and Deployment* being the title of a report published as long ago as 1988 (GS Misc 858), has seldom been out of the spotlight since then and it is hardly surprising that Clergy often find themselves at a loss as to exactly what is being asked and expected of them. One default position is to reinforce the priority of Priesthood with important books by

Michael Ramsey, Robert Martineau, Wesley Carr and John Pritchard continuing to provide inspiration and encouragement in changing times. Another default position is common but far less healthy. This manifests itself when Clergy adopt a policy of retrenchment by seeking to maintain traditional patterns of working which are inherently unsustainable, and trying to meet expectations which are patently unrealistic. In this latter respect they are likely to be colluding with unreasonable and unreconstructed expectations of parishioners who believe they have a professional holy person in their midst who should be able to be relied on to meet their relentless requirements and to be answerable to them in all respects. Whilst Wesley Carr has been right to affirm the role of the Clergy as recipients of all kinds of projections in their exercise of the priest-like task, this is not the same as trying to meet irresponsible expectations which are damaging to the well-being of Clergy, their families and those whose genuine needs consequently go unaddressed. (See Sara Savage: "On the Analyst's Couch: Psychological Perspectives on Congregations and Clergy" in *The Future of the Parish System*. Steven Croft (Ed.) Church House Publishing 2006 pp. 16 – 32).

Now my feeling is that both the misbegotten expectations of parishioners – Churchgoers and non-Churchgoers alike – and the readiness of Clergy to try and meet them are relics of religion insofar as they are about the things of God being harnessed to the performance of functions rather than the flourishing of faith. Perhaps too much has been made of "being there" as virtually the be-all and end-all of ministry. But it is an antidote to the treadmill of religious duties which can prove so enervating to the life of faith, and there are times when Clergy need to be told: don't just do something, stand there! After all, the risen Jesus first of all stood amongst His disciples before speaking to them a word of peace and empowering them with the gift of the Holy Spirit (John 20 vss 19 – 23). As the boundary markers between "ministers of religion" and "the faithful" become less and less pronounced, and more and more of the people of God, by virtue of their Baptism, share in meeting expectations which traditionally have been borne by the Clergy it will be by faith rather than by Office that ministry and mission will be taken forward into the future. Thereby those in Ordained ministry will be clear as to their role in fostering faith in themselves and others so that as all are called, all are challenged and equipped to serve according to their gifts and opportunities. Clergy will need a good deal of support and some re-training if they are to avoid the default positions, and so subvert the immature dependency culture which religion tends to reinforce and from which faith in God seeks to release us. But it is a calling consistent with the Great Commission and one which can be embraced with renewed confidence and commitment.

But what might the Church look like when we move on from the rather severe divide between "ministers of religion" on the one hand and "the faithful" on the other? My hope and expectation is that it will be humble enough to build on the past where appropriate, brave enough to strike out on a new path when necessary, and wise enough to know the difference.

Let us look first at what we have inherited and how and where it might continue to be serviceable for showing and sharing the good news of Christ now and in the years ahead.

The Church of England's parochial system has rested historically on three key principles:

For every person a Parish;
For every Parish a parson;
For every parson a payment.

It has now been the case for many years that not all parsons receive payment, and there has been a significant growth in non-stipendiary Ordained ministry and voluntary local Lay ministry.

So the third key principle has been significantly modified.

The same cannot be said of the first principle, which remains central to our role as the Church of the nation. Everyone lives in a Parish whether or not they know or care, and everyone enjoys rights in relation to their Parish Church when it comes to e.g. Baptisms, Weddings and Funerals.

This leaves the second principle which continues to hold, but in ways which many of our predecessors would find difficult to recognise. So whilst every Parish has a designated parson, they might well be sharing that parson with several other Parishes. This is especially the case in rural areas. On the other hand, they may be in a Team Ministry so that two or more parsons might have a care for them.

So the Anglican parochial vision is evolving, and it is evident that the second principle in particular is set to evolve further.

The word "parson" effectively conveys the sense of a persona i.e. a person who represents a community to God and God to that community. It is not essential for such a parson, or persona, to be Ordained even if historically that has generally been the case. In many places already – and especially in multi-Parish Benefices – local lay people are fulfilling this role. Of course it relates closely to the role of Churchwarden, but it need not and often it is not the Churchwarden who serves in this way. Within such a scenario there is renewed scope for the development of a distinctive Diaconate.

There is a great deal to be said for holding on to the vision of: for every Parish a parson. So our evolving vision looks towards every community having its parson / persona, Ordained or Lay, paid or voluntary who is equipped and authorised to exercise such a representative ministerial role for and with those amongst whom they live, work and worship day by day. But they will be modelling more than ministry in this persona role; they will also be witnessing to discipleship in daily life where the Church engages with the world and vice-versa.

All this has profound implications for the Ordained ministry. Because many or even most of the people fulfilling the persona role in their communities will be lay, it will be vital to ensure the availability of sufficient Priests to offer distinctively Priestly ministry where and when it is needed. Whilst the local persona will, with others, be able to ensure that worship is offered in every community week by week, and even prayers said in Church day by day, the importance of the people of God gathering for Eucharist on a regular basis is beyond question, as is the need for a reliable ministry of reconciliation and benediction.

Stipendiary Clergy will be crucial to this evolution of the parochial system. They will have an increasingly episcopal role in nurturing ministry and discipleship, and in working collegially and collaboratively with the persona people and other local lay leaders. Special skills will be required to realise the potential and attend to the well-being of those who are essentially volunteers. Being there for these people in a supportive, prayerful and resourceful way will be more important than responding to demands which can be met by other means. As with Bishops, stipendiary Clergy in such roles will continue to exercise priestly ministry but it will be to the ministry of oversight and encouragement that they will chiefly devote themselves. Much of this resonates with the Tiller Report which has proved to be remarkably prophetic in so many ways. Furthermore, it shows how it might be possible to build upon and evolve what has served this country well for a thousand years.

However, it has its limitations. Whilst the idea of a persona in every parish might enable our parochial system to remain serviceable, this is only likely to be possible in rural areas. Even there we face the challenge of new housing developments which are often at least semi-detached from the historic village and its community life – including the Churches. Meanwhile, the environs of market towns and the suburbs of cities sprout enormous developments which boast little by way of infrastructure and where parish boundaries are more or less irrelevant. Once we add in the inner-city areas where traditional patterns of Church presence are under severe strain, and also take on board the implications of today's increasingly mobile and networked society, we quickly realise that the persona model of ministry cannot be entertained. In one Deanery in rural Shropshire one per cent of the adult population is a Churchwarden. There is an adult population of 6,000 with 30 Parish Churches served by 60 Wardens. Now compare that with an urban parish of 10,000 people where it is unlikely that 100 people would be found to fulfil such a role. In terms of how we organise ourselves as a Church, we are in two different worlds, and if rural areas might still sustain an evolved version of the parish system based on faithful volunteers supported by a reducing number of stipendiary Clergy, this simply will not be possible elsewhere and we will need to effect a paradigm shift in our strategies for ministry and mission.

This is where the Chaplaincy model of ministry might prove fruitful. It is usual for Chaplains to indwell places which are transitory in terms of population, and those to whom they minister will usually have their centre of gravity elsewhere. So they may live or work there for the time being, but sooner or later they will return home to somewhere else. If there is a Chapel it will be an adjunct to the Chaplaincy rather than, as with Parish Churches in relation to their Clergy, the other way round. Chaplains indwell places in ways which impact on their ethos, and although they may be called upon to perform particular functions on a regular basis, they will generally be skilled at being present to people graciously and unobtrusively. It is a tribute to the way in which Chaplains fulfil their role that whereas management bodies of hospitals or colleges may challenge their presence on religious or financial grounds, staff and residents usually lobby hard to retain their services.

Somehow Chaplains are seen not as religious functionaries but as points of contact with dimensions of faith and spirituality which still matter to people, even when contact with organised religion is little or non-existent.

In many ways new housing areas and leisure or work-based networks offer the same kind of challenges and opportunities as are met by Chaplains on a regular basis. They are transitory in terms of population and temporary when it comes to any sense of belonging or community spirit. The existence or otherwise of a specifically set-apart Church building will matter less than knowing that someone is there for them on a regular and reliable basis to resource and encourage their own expressions of Church. They will expect to be largely self-sufficient in relation to how and where they worship, witness and offer pastoral care. However, they will derive comfort and confidence from knowing that a suitably skilled person is accompanying them as they seek to be faithful in sometimes apathetic or even hostile circumstances. As with their counterparts in more familiar Chaplaincy situations, these Chaplains will be perceived to be not so much ministers of religion as pathfinders for faith where the traditional religious landmarks no longer show the way.

Much of this is already being worked on in the aftermath of the *Mission-Shaped Church* Report and the introduction of Pioneer Ministers. However, there are already signs that the dead hand of religion is getting a grip on these initiatives so that no end of regulations, guidelines and codes of practice are in place to rein in more flamboyant flights of faith. The times are urgent, and if there are going to be fields ripe for harvest then seeds will need to be sown in what are rapidly becoming vast tracts of uncharted territory as far as the Church is concerned. Wherever we seek to take the good news of God forward into the future, we can be confident that ministering religion will no longer be effective, even if ever it was. Mobilising all people of faith and goodwill, supported by equally faithful ministers called, commissioned and fit for purpose will be crucial to ensuring that religion is servant not master of the Church we cherish and the faith we proclaim.

We now need to address head on whether this privileging of people of faith over ministers of religion merely colludes with what Andrew Keen calls *The Cult of the Amateur* (Brearley Publishing 2007). Keen's challenge is all the more pertinent because it emerges from his background in internet technology which he now accuses of "killing our culture". His Damascene conversion was not on the Road to Damascus but on a camping trip to Sebastopol, a small farming town just north of California's Silicon Valley. Sebastopol is the headquarters of O'Reilly Media, a market leader in the promotion of information technology. The terms in which Keen goes on to describe O'Reilly media are surely significant: "an evangelizer of innovation to a worldwide congregation of technophiles. It is Silicon Valley's most fervent preacher" (p. 12). When we set this alongside Keen's description of Wikipedia as "the Internet's largest cathedral of knowledge" (p. 20) and his reference to Google, "with its Ministry of Truth credo of *Do No Evil*" (p. 182) we are left in no doubt that he sees the Internet in as much religious as cultural terms. This is confirmed by his commentary on Google co-founder Larry Page's dream of the "ultimate" search engine which, according to Page, "would understand everything in the world. It would understand everything that you asked it and give you back the exact right thing instantly". This, says Keen "is Google's holy grail. Its the modern-day version of the ancient Greek oracle. Its the Judaeo-Christian idea of an omnipotent, omnipresent God" (p. 183). By no means least, Keen sees the Internet usurping the role of mainstream religion evidenced symbolically by sites such as sermoncentral.com, sermonspice.com and desperatepreacher.com being accessed more and more by preachers in search of sermons they can plagiarise without effort or acknowledgement (p. 144).

Whilst we need to remind ourselves that printed sermons have been in circulation virtually since the invention of printing itself, and preachers have often found them to be their salvation when bereft of time or ideas, still we must take seriously Keen's contention that the ideological implications of the Internet owe a great deal to the realms of spirituality, theology and religious commitment – and perhaps offer another example alongside the cult of consumerism described in a previous chapter, of how readily religion can be co-opted and colonised by socio-cultural projects pursuing agendas which are controversial or even sinister in their implications.

However, the crucial issue raised by Keen from our point of view is explicit in the title of his book which, of course, also contains a word with religious significance: *The Cult of the Amateur*. The issue is sharpened for us by the way in which the terms "amateur" and "lay" are often used synonymously. When we see the future of Christianity as majoring on the work and witness of faithful lay persons rather than traditional, but no less faithful, ministers of religion are we subscribing to this cult of the amateur? To answer this question we need to delve deeper into the causes of Keen's anxiety, and the options available to address them.

George Bernard Shaw once said, "Hell is full of amateur musicians" but today, says Keen "Shaw's hell would have broadband access and would be overrun with bloggers and podcasters" (p. 36). The so-called democratization of knowledge and opinion which has been hailed by Internet entrepreneurs as finally subverting "the tyranny of expertise" is in fact heralding "the decline of the quality and reliability of the information we receive, thereby distorting, if not outrightly corrupting, our national civic conversation" (p. 27). When what one person knows is deemed to be qualitatively equivalent to what everyone else knows, and one opinion is as good as any other, then those who are valued as particularly wise and knowing in society will have their credentials neutralised and their contribution discounted. We are then reminded of T. S. Eliot's *cri de coeur*: "Where is the wisdom we have lost in knowledge? Where is the knowledge we have lost in information?" (Choruses from *The Rock* (1934)). A laudable attempt to empower the amateur has the (possibly) unintended consequence that wells of creative genius and imagination run dry for lack of appropriate encouragement, resourcing and affirmation. Where there are no experts, all are amateurs, and where Wikipedia meets MySpace meets YouTube we are captive to what Keen calls the law of digital Darwinism, "the survival of the loudest and most opinionated" (p. 15).

Now it has to be said that Keen displays much of the almost fanatical zeal of the convert. He is reluctant to see anything of value on the Internet, and he does look at the past through rose-tinted spectacles. After all, when we look back upon how the intellectual, social and political life of western culture has been dominated by male, moneyed and middle to upper class citizens it can hardly be said that "the survival of the loudest and most opinionated" is an innovation of the World Wide Web. Furthermore, what James Surowiecki has called "the wisdom of crowds" has all too often been set at nought by an over emphasis on expert opinion (see James Surowiecki: *The Wisdom of Crowds: Why the Many are Smarter than the Few and How Collective Wisdom Shapes Business, Economics, Societies and Nations* (Doubleday 2004). Maybe, to paraphrase the cynical Dean in Tom Sharpe's *Porterhouse Blue*, "if a little knowledge is a dangerous thing, just imagine how much damage a lot of it could do!"

More recently Don Tapscott and Anthony D. Williams have predicted the demise of large corporations once experts are networked world-wide on the Web, and paid for their contributions, so that the expert guidance advocated by Keen and the wisdom of crowds commended by Surowieck; can be cunningly co-ordinated. (*Wikinomics: How Mass Collaboration Changes Everything*. Atlantic Books 2007).

Yet the implications of a "cult of the amateur" are very serious, and are already being felt by traditional media for the dissemination of news, comment, opinion and information. When such dissemination has been thoroughly democratized, and the Internet becomes the sole means whereby we access the world beyond ourselves, how much will we be able to rely on the truthfulness, authenticity and credibility of what we are being told? Trust in the reliability of even the best of journalism and public service broadcasting is already at a low ebb, but it is hardly likely to be rescued by resort to blogs and podcasts of dubious provenance and untested intelligence. This may be seen by some as a surreal scenario, but such is the declared ambition of leaders in the Internet industry so that Richard Edelman, Chief Executive of the world's largest privately owned public relations company can confirm that "in this era of exploding media technologies there is no truth except the truth you create for yourself" (Keen *op.cit.* p. 17).

Clearly the trend towards the development and deployment of lay people of faith as key to the future of Christian mission and ministry in this country has as one of its drivers the same empowerment motive as inspires the gurus of the Internet. The professionalization of the Clergy has brought many benefits, but it has also been seen as disabling of faithful lay people who are often complicit in their own subordination to "the tyranny of expertise". Giving lay people a voice in the government of the Church, for example, and providing opportunities for the discernment and deployment of their gifts has balanced a perceived overemphasis on clerical authority and qualifications to minister. Liberating the laity has concentrated the minds of many seeking to realise a less hierarchical and more New Testament vision for organised Christianity in the 21st Century. Reliance on ministers of religion, who at worst infantilize lay people, and at best patronize them, is giving way to the freeing up of the faithful to fulfil their God-given potential. So the argument goes, and it is not only the syndics of Silicon Valley who welcome this as a long overdue corrective to the power of religious professionals. If there is too much religion in the world, and not enough faith, then this is one way to put that right.

But Keen's challenge to the champions of the Internet is also a challenge to the Churches. Charges of dumbing down Christianity at the expense of theological rigour and sound scholarship are already prevalent, and whatever the rhetoric of those responsible for selecting and training the Church's ministers there is a lurking suspicion that standards are on the slide when it comes to who can be authorised to teach, preach and prophesy in the name of the Lord. Is "the cult of the amateur" in danger of infecting the Churches as well, so that a profession of faith becomes the crucial criterion for proclaiming the truth? In reaction to the rigours of religion, is there a relaxation of standards such that accreditation for ministry becomes democratized and communicating the truths of revelation and tradition is consequentially compromised?

In relation to the Internet, Keen seeks to rein in the more radical ambitions of its most ideological advocates by resisting a revolution in information technology whilst recommending reform of our inherited media of communication exchange. A role must be found for the "experts" to act as guardians of what can be relied on as truth, and gatekeepers of informed and intelligent opinion. For example, Larry Sanger of Wikipedia has explored ways "to incorporate the voice and authority of experts with user-generated content". He called it Citizendium, and launched in 2006, Sanger describes it as "an experimental new wiki project that combines public participation with gentle expert guidance". Keen believes this platform "will enable professional content producers to combine the traditional one-to-many broadcasting functionality of network television with the many-to-many interactivity of online content". This way we might be able "to balance the best of the digital future without destroying the institutions of the past" (Keen p. 186 and 188). Whether this experiment can or will succeed remains to be seen. But the very fact that the attempt is being made serves to underline the extent to which absolute reliance on an unsupervised and unregulated network of amateur online bloggers and podcasters is perceived to be potentially dangerous and unsustainable.

James Martin takes up this theme in *The Meaning of the 21st Century: a vital blueprint for ensuring our future.* (Transworld 2007 pp. 407 – 9):

"Electronic technologies are causing humankind to accumulate an overwhelming deluge of digital material. The deluge will become larger at a rapidly accelerating rate. This global deluge will be searched by Googles of the future. As it grows, an important question becomes, 'How do you find the good-quality items in the vast ocean of sludge?'. We will need the ability to separate the sheep from the goats, because as the deluge progresses there may be one sheep for a million goats. ... Digital civilization will be global and will have an ever-growing and ultimately overwhelming quantity of data and products. This is tenable only if there are strong means of quality control. Processes of refinement and enhancement need to go on continuously, distilling out the best and improving it and hiding the worst. Without such processes, we'll all be drowning in an ocean of mediocrity."

Likewise, the role of religion and those we have come to categorise as ministers of religion, will continue to be vital in a Church where the ministry of the whole People of God is being mustered and mobilised. What Sanger describes as "gentle expert guidance" will ensure that people of faith can realise their potential as called and gifted by God, without assuming the mantle of the religious professional whose institutional defensiveness and proprietorial tendencies can so often serve to dampen down any spark of faith rather than fanning it into a flame. At its best such "gentle expert guidance" will exemplify the role of religion in the service of faith. Professional theologians and full-time Stipendiary Clergy will be needed as never before to equip, support, guide and monitor an ever larger number of lay people duly authorised to represent their community to God and God to their community. After all, the wisdom of crowds is far from infallible, and when each does what is wise in their own eyes the results are not always edifying. Just as digital technology has opened up positive and unprecedented ways in which we can globally connect and share information, so the liberation of the laity holds out hope for the full flowering of faith. But in both cases the cult of the amateur needs to be mitigated by the wisdom of the wise and the cleverness of the clever, because only then can people of faith be truly fools for Christ (I Corinthians chapter 4 vs 10).

Crisis? What Crisis?

"Atheism itself can become a conceptual idol, a fixed position as belligerent as theism, which is why evangelical atheists and evangelical theists could be said to deserve each other". (Richard Holloway).

"Mr. Prettiman] demonstrates to the thoughtful eye how really irrational a rationalist philosopher can be". (William Golding: *Rites of Passage*).

"It's not the existence of God we're bothered about but the existence of you who say you believe in him". (Andrew O'Hagan: *Be Near Me*).

Why is the leading Baptist Church in Lincoln named after one of the most out-spoken secularist freethinkers of the 19th Century? For sure, Thomas Cooper was raised in Gainsborough which is a Lincolnshire town, and as a Wesleyan local preacher he ministered in Lincoln in the 1820's. But during a spell in prison after being convicted of inciting disorder in support of the Chartist cause, he developed a deep religious scepticism and he soon became a popular speaker in the main freethinking halls in London. George Holyoake, by then the premier Secularist leader affirmed that Cooper was "incomparably the most attractive of our metropolitan lecturers" (Robert Conklin: Thomas Cooper, *The Chartist*. Manilla 1935 p. 374).

As with many who are identified with the 19th Century "crisis of faith", Cooper retained affection and admiration for the character and teaching of Jesus whilst rejecting all the miraculous and supernaturalist claims made by orthodox Christians. He was much influenced by D. F. Strauss whose *Leben Jesu* was translated by George Eliot as *The Life of Christ Critically Examined* (1846).

Here the Gospel narratives are subjected to the kind of critical analysis which seriously undermined confidence in the coherence and reliability of scripture. Furthermore, Strauss sought to refute or explain away all the supernatural dimensions of the Jesus story so that what is left is a fine example of a human being, but nothing more. Out went any belief in the Virgin Birth or the Resurrection, as did doctrines of Atonement and life after death. Cooper seriously doubted whether anyone who really thought the issues through could possibly believe the teachings of orthodox Christianity. In his journal he wrote: "I wonder how any man can hold by orthodoxy when he has once dared to think for himself" (*Cooper's Journal*. London 1850 p. 459).

In the promulgation of such views, Cooper was in the company of those who became identified with what A. N. Wilson has described as *God's Funeral* (W. W. Norton 1999). The "melancholy long withdrawing roar" of the sea of faith from *Dover Beach* as recounted by Matthew Arnold in his poem of 1851, caught many in its flow. There was Frederic Young who, like Cooper, had been a lay preacher and who, on losing his faith, became a founding member of the London Secular Society in 1853. To doubts raised by the findings of biblical criticism he added challenges posed by evolutionary science and concerns about the moral and social teaching of scripture, especially concerning the rights of women. Then there was John Henry Gordon who added to the usual mix of motives for religious scepticism a dose of trenchant anticlericalism which caused quite a stir in his native Carlisle. In 1861 he published *The Exodus of Priests: A Secularist's Dream of Better Times* in which he foresaw a utopia where in 1960's Britain people will have forsaken spiritual remedies and theological speculations and, instead, concentrate on practical, attainable knowledge: "Thus, instead of praying God not to send fever among them, the people take care not to breed it in their midst" (*op.cit.* p. 2). By no means least, there was Joseph Barker who turned his back on a promising career as a

Christian preacher and polemicist when he became attracted to the arguments of sceptics who challenged the integrity of scripture, the authority of Church leaders and the social values of Christian orthodoxy. After an excursion into radical politics, with religion well in his sights as one of the main causes of poverty and injustice, he emigrated to America where he quickly became a freethinking leader of national prominence. He returned to England for lecture tours to great acclaim before moving back permanently in 1860 where he was welcomed with open arms by the community of organised atheists. Cooper, Young, Gordon and Barker – this list gets longer as we add the names of John Bebbington, George Sexton, Charles Southwell and James Spilling.

Now, for all the differences between them, there are two main features they have in common. The first of these is that between them they not only aggregate the sum of sceptical arguments which characterised atheistic secularism in the 19th Century, but they are almost entirely the same arguments as are recycled by 21st Century sceptics led by Richard Dawkins in *The God Delusion* (Transworld 2006). Like Dawkins, they found little to re-assure them in the traditional proofs for the existence of God and had little compunction about lining up with Kant and Hume to debunk them. They agreed with Dawkins that the conclusions of biblical criticism effectively discredited the Gospels as historical records, whilst they concluded with Randolph Churchill on reading the Old Testament: "God, isn't God a shit!" – quoted, of course, with relish by Dawkins (p. 51). They asserted the autonomy of ethics over against claims that morality required religion if it is to be sustainable. This argument is also deployed by Dawkins, and although he is less inclined towards the kinds of personalised anticlericalism characteristic of 19th Century polemics, he does agree with his forebears that the moral stance of the Churches in relation to e.g. homosexuality, the rights of women and advances in medical science leaves much to be desired.

Of course, the centre-piece of Dawkins' case against God rests on Darwinian evolution and the principle of natural selection. He acknowledges the awesome complexity of the universe, but does not accept that the only options by way of explanation are intelligent design on the one hand, or chance on the other. Taken as a whole, the improbability of the universe coming together as it is other than by design seems too great to allow for any alternative explanation. However, when the process of natural selection is reduced to its constituent stages over billions of years each stage becomes far less improbable and therefore more explicable in terms of natural science, with supernaturalist hypotheses no longer required. Reducible complexity replaces God as the ultimate explanation for all that is and is to come. Of course, the theist is not actually seen off by this compelling but crucially incomplete thesis as is well demonstrated by Keith Ward (*Why There Almost Certainly is a God*. Lion 2008) and John Cornwell (*Darwin's Angel*. Profile Books 2007). However, whilst the scientific sceptics of the 19th Century may not have been able to develop Darwin's findings to the sophisticated level attained by today's scientists, they quickly saw the implications for Christianity and the Churches as a result of biblical accounts of creation being evidentially undermined. As yet they had not seen how biblical criticism would itself help to clarify matters by showing scripture to be rather more theological and poetical than scientific in its purpose and composition. This had to await the emergence of modernism and liberalism as the century progressed. However, they would have recognised the fundamental thrust of Dawkins' argument just as he would see them as his forefathers in the confrontation with faith. And there is a great deal in what he has to say with which many Christians would want to agree. But just as with arguments for the existence of God, arguments against may be cumulatively impressive but none of them are individually persuasive. And as ten leaky buckets hold no more water than one leaky bucket, it may simply boil down to whose buckets leak least! As is so often the case, Dawkins is right in what he affirms and wrong in what he denies. Or, to put that another way, he is right about most things that matter but wrong about the things which matter most.

Our purpose in engaging with Dawkins at this point has been to line him up alongside those 19th Century exemplars of that "crisis of faith" which most commentators on Victorian England assume to be the only show in town so far as religion was concerned. The arguments for atheism which they marshal and deploy are effectively the same as are being aired today, and this is the first thing that Thomas Cooper and his sceptical colleagues had in common.

But the second shared characteristic is even more significant. Because far from actually being exemplars of a crisis of faith, they were just a few amongst many whom Timothy Larsen describes in *Crisis of Doubt: Honest Faith in Nineteenth Century England* (OUP 2006). For what Cooper, Young, Barker and the rest had in common was that they returned to the Christian faith – they reconverted. As Larsen demonstrates, a far greater percentage of Secularist leaders became Christian than Christian Ministers became sceptics. Indeed, this caused repeated convulsions in the freethinking movement which had to put "spin" into overdrive when these defections occurred so as to defame the turncoats and limit the damage. Yet amongst these re-converts were some of those who were held in the highest regard by Holyoake, and were entrusted with lecturing extensively on behalf of the Secularist cause as well as writing for, and even editing, radical journals. It was not easy to declare them to be of good learning and sound mind one minute, and then declare them to be intellectually unstable and emotionally immature the next. But attitudes to apostasy always being what they are, these characters were subject to a great deal of abuse and vilification such that we have to ask what were the reasons which caused them to reconvert, and do these reasons continue to remain cogent in the context of current crises of faith and alleged delusions?

Meanwhile, Thomas Cooper returned to Lincoln in later life "going out in his 76th year to preach Christianity to which he is devoted" (Conklin *op.cit.* pp. 460 – 1). It is a tribute to Holyoake that in Cooper's case he forbore to attack his erstwhile ally but successfully petitioned Gladstone to give him a pension – and it is a tribute to Cooper that a Church in Lincoln still stands to his memory.

Larsen suggests numerous reasons why leading Secularists faced a "crisis of doubt" and eventually reconverted. The following seem to have been most prevalent and decisive:

1. Scepticism was experienced as negative and destructive with nothing offered as an alternative to faith as a philosophy or positive world view by which to live.

2. Whilst sceptics generally lived according to decent moral principles, this was believed by the reconverts to be because they had been brought up in a Christian environment – morally, they were running on borrowed fuel. They saw little in secularism by way of a sustainable rationale for why acts were deemed right or wrong. They sensed a strain of moral anarchy in what they were leaving behind.

3. The importance of reason was not disputed by the reconverts, but they now saw more clearly that humanity has other sources of knowledge, identified with terms such as heart, instincts, feeling and inwardness. Secularism was accused of relegating these sources of knowledge to an unacceptable level.

4. Reconverts came to see that they had adopted a far too simplistic view of Scripture during their secularist phase. As a resource of Revelation the Bible needed to be apprehended in far more sensitive and sophisticated ways.

5. Even as atheists, those who underwent a crisis of faith still retained respect and admiration for the figure of Jesus of Nazareth. The Gospels painted a picture so compelling that only an historical original could account for it. To a significant extent the reconverts were drawn back to God by Jesus.

6. Although many of the reconverts were accused by their former co-sceptics of being motivated by money, publicity or emotionalism, they were mostly disadvantaged financially and in terms of public profile by embracing Christianity. Furthermore, the main reasons why they reconverted were intellectual rather than emotional. They were impressed by the intelligence and intellectual brilliance of leading Christians with whom they debated either on stage or in print. "In the end", says Larsen, "they were able to give learned explanations in which they articulated why they no longer found their former [sceptical] convictions compelling. ... [the] reconverts were thinking Victorians who were intellectually honest" (op.cit. p. 244).

Of course, those who reconverted did not find themselves back exactly where they started. They had rejected Christianity for a range of reasons, and their motives for returning to the fold were equally mixed. However, it is fair to say on the basis of the definitions we have offered for "religion" and "faith" respectively that what they had rejected was the Christian religion, and what they subsequently embraced was the Christian faith. The formalism of religion entailed degrees of biblical fundamentalism, doctrinal dogmatism, moral authoritarianism, institutional conservatism and anti-scientific obscurantism, which their credulity could no longer bear. On the other hand, they found that atheism not only failed to fill the gap left by their erstwhile religious convictions, but fulfilment could only be found in a faith freed from the tendentious tenets of religion which the sceptics had rightly rejected but for which scepticism could provide no satisfying or sustainable substitute.

This is the point at which Richard Dawkins can be re-introduced into our considerations. After all, if his reasons for declaring God to be a delusion are much the same as those which triggered the 19th Century "crisis of faith", then we can ask whether factors which fuelled the less regarded but equally significant "crisis of doubt" might apply to him and to others as well.

First of all, we pointed to the destructive tendencies of scepticism and the failure to provide satisfactory alternatives to faith as a positive world view by which to live. Dawkins is right to insist that passionate protest against the worst excesses, inconsistencies and abuses of religion should not be muted on account of believers feelings and sensibilities. Religion can never be above or beyond criticism. However, it is legitimate to ask what framework of meaning the sceptic proposes to build in place of what has been dismantled. For Dawkins the answer lies in evolutionary science and the imperative of reducible complexity. Yet for all his infectious enthusiasm, immense learning and fine communication skills we are left to ponder whether "reducible complexity" is sufficient to capture the essence of awe and wonder which for people of faith finds expression in worship and praise. Those caught up in the Victorian "crisis of doubt" found little in atheism to re-furnish their faith – and Dawkins' scientific positivism fares no better.

As for morality, Dawkins legitimately exposes and condemns much that has been taught and perpetrated by religions of all kinds down the ages. He gleefully lights upon many parts of the Bible which liberal Christians find as distasteful and unacceptable as he does. He has no difficulty showing how, in many respects, Christians and non-Christians behave in equally moral or immoral ways. In fact, because of the religious convictions which are invoked to justify them, many evils have been perpetrated by believers far more severe than even the most devout sceptic would ever contemplate. (See, for example, A. C. Grayling: *The Choice of Hercules.* Phoenix 2007). Yet Dawkins' espousal of "The Moral Zeitgeist" as a rationale for morality is highly speculative with values chronically relativised and in a constant state of flux. He may well have demonstrated how attempts by religion to dictate and codify morality are destined to fall foul of the actual behaviour of its adherents, but he has not thereby displaced faith as morality's key and cornerstone. Richard Holloway has made a robust case for "Keeping Religion out of Ethics" (the sub-title of *Godless Morality.* Canongate. Edinburgh 1999) but, on our definition, Faith remains very much in play.

Thirdly, Dawkins pays appropriate tribute to Peter Atkins whose *Creation Revisited* (OUP 1992) he describes as "my favourite work of prose poetry" (Dawkins *op.cit.* p. 143). If anything, Atkins excels even this high standard in *Galileo's Finger* (OUP 2006) which is a wonderfully *poetic* account of *science.* Yet we are left wondering whether he, or anyone else for that matter, would be able to supply such a satisfying *scientific* account of *poetry.* Like those 19th Century predecessors, Dawkins is a child of the Enlightenment so that his scepticism, like theirs, is essentially founded upon Reason and the challenges posed by rationalism to all kinds of religion and supernaturalism. But as we have seen, many of them came to the conclusion that Christianity can be embraced on intellectual and rational grounds without compromising the claims of heart and soul to convey truths which are more the stuff of poetry than scientific analysis. Religion must be prepared to face up to the seriousness of Dawkins' rational and scientific critique – it simply cannot respond by turning up the volume on its repertoire of revealed truths. But faith which loves God not only with strength of mind, but of heart and soul as well, stands to be enriched rather than undermined by the revelations of Darwin, Dawkins *et al*. Gillian Evans puts it well:

> " 'What can a reasonable person believe' is a question full of unexpected turnings and hidden places where unforeseen forms of 'reasonableness' have been 'discovered'. This need not make the modern enquirer nervous, but it should make him or her resistant to being persuaded that belief is somehow unworthy or old-fashioned or unscientific because it is 'unreasonable'." (*op.cit.* p. 10).

Fourthly, Thomas Cooper and his colleagues felt the full force of the challenge to biblical authority posed by D. F. Strauss and the newly emerging tools of Historical Criticism. Taken together with scientific evidence as to the true age of the planet these tools chipped away at the Pentateuch as a whole and Genesis in particular. Discrepancies in and between the Gospels were mercilessly exposed as evidence of human artifice rather than divine revelation. Textual criticism raised questions about whether we could ever arrive at a definitive version of Scripture which could be confidently proclaimed as the Word of the Lord. Many freethinkers latched on to these findings of biblical scholarship as the main weapons in their exposure of religion as fraudulent and discredited. Dawkins also pursues this line of attack, but with far less justification. For example, he makes merry with the very different and historically incompatible accounts of the birth of Jesus in the Gospels of Matthew and Luke. But he knows full well that mainstream New Testament scholarship sees these texts as fairly sophisticated theological constructs which almost certainly share key data in common from the tradition they inherited, but which have it as their main purpose to illuminate the Person of Christ rather than provide eyewitness accounts of the nativity. Yet even without the benefit of more recent developments in biblical theology and historiography the 19th Century reconverts came to appreciate that the Bible was a far more subtle witness to God and God's purposes than either the proponents of religious orthodoxy which they had rejected, or the sceptical critics they had subsequently joined, were prepared to admit. But their newfound faith had little difficulty in accommodating and even celebrating the fruits of biblical criticism which still seem beyond the reach of the fundamentalists Dawkins quite properly condemns, but from which sceptics might well derive nourishment once the true nature of the Bible is understood and appreciated.

Fifthly, even the most trenchant opponents of the Christian religion have been inclined to retain respect for Jesus as a teacher and moral exemplar. This was certainly true for the Victorian sceptics, and those who reconverted generally cite a renewed respect for Jesus and His divinity as a crucial factor. Whilst Dawkins concedes that Jesus "probably existed" he rejects C. S. Lewis' argument that He was "Mad, Bad or God" (Dawkins *op.cit.*p. 117). He suggests that Jesus "was honestly mistaken", and we might detect at least a glimmer of admiration for the heroic figure who is to be found somewhere beneath the accretions of religious propaganda which obscure, according to the sceptics, the Jesus of history. Certainly Dawkins takes some ironic pleasure in his "Atheists for Jesus" T-Shirt. If those in times past who rejected the Jesus of religion found their way back to belief in God through the Jesus of faith, then who is to say this might not be possible for the sceptics of today?

Finally, our cohort of reconverts were impressed by the intellectual stature of many theists who withstood the much vaunted "crisis of faith". Whilst Dawkins calls into question the number of scientists who are claimed to be theists, he cannot plausibly argue, as many did in the 19th Century, that faith can only be embraced by those who are intellectually challenged. There are simply too many examples of highly intelligent people who profess belief in God, and amongst them the Pope and the

Archbishop of Canterbury might reasonably be described as two of the most intellectually gifted people in Europe. Dawkins graciously acknowledges the intellectual stature of Bishop Richard Harries amongst others with whom he has found himself in debate on matters of faith. This needs to be remembered because there is a tendency, particularly in the popular Press, to equate belief in God with some form of mental deficiency. This is plainly not the case, and if religion sometimes seems to require people to leave their brains at the door when going to worship God, this has never been consistent with the kind of coherent and enquiring faith which Cooper, Young and Barker eventually embraced after their aborted excursions into scepticism. There is simply too much of that kind of religion in the world, and not enough of that kind of faith. May intelligent believers be as instrumental in countering scepticism in the 21st Century as they were when the so-called "crisis of faith" was convulsing Victorian England.

As himself a kind of reconvert in the 21st Century, John Cornwell does a good line in turning the tables on Dawkins when it comes to pursuing the latter's arguments to their logical conclusion. Attempts to classify religious faith, however mild or "sensible" (to use Dawkins' word), as evidence of mental malfunctioning has profound socio-political implications for which the totalitarian regimes of the 20th Century offer ample evidence. Furthermore, by raising the rhetoric of atheism to near hysterical levels Dawkins is inviting religious fundamentalists to batten down the hatches and become even more fundamentalist in the face of a totally intolerant scientism (John Cornwell: *Darwin's Angel: An Angelic Riposte to the God Delusion*. Profile 2007). This is why Dawkins is often described as himself a fundamentalist – a label he resists by protesting that he is merely "passionate" about the primacy of science and the unsustainability of supernaturalism (Dawkins *op.cit.* pp. 319 – 323). Dawkins is certainly not a fundamentalist according to the definition offered by Malise Ruthven. What he calls "the F word" is defined as:

> "a religious way of being that manifests itself in a strategy by which beleaguered believers attempt to preserve their distinctive identity as a people or group in the face of modernity and secularisation" (Malise Ruthven: *Fundamentalism: The Search for Meaning* OUP 2004 p. 8).

However, if Dawkins is passionate, then it is the passion of the evangelist. Perhaps it is more appropriate to describe Dawkins as an evangelist insofar as he is passionate about what he believes (or doesn't believe) and wants others to believe it (or not) as well. Certainly Clare George's clever novel *The Evangelist* about "a charismatic, passionate champion of reason and science" could have had Dawkins at least partly in mind (Sceptre 2005. See also: Tina Beattie *The New Atheists*. DLT 2007).

From our point of view, the really tantalising issues are to do with the relative status of religion and faith when we compare the "crises" of faith and doubt in the 19th Century with our current skirmishes with scepticism. As we have seen, whilst Cooper & Co turned against Christianity and fulminated against it with a vehemence which matches anything seen today, it was essentially against the formalising of faith that they were protesting. In other words, they were actually rejecting religion and, with it, the faith which had become subservient to its purposes. But what brought them back to faith was a recovery of Faith itself. As Larsen puts it:

> "a focus on the crisis of doubt of plebeian radicals in the nineteenth century provides a fresh perspective on the intellectual resilience and cogency of faith in general and Christianity in particular in the Victorian period" (*op.cit.* p. 253).

Are there pointers here to how things might work out for Faith in the future? It is not for us to predict how Richard Dawkins' attitudes to Religion and Faith might develop given his assurance that "I know what it would take to change my mind, and I would gladly do so if the necessary evidence were forthcoming". There are enough controls in there to ensure that his mind remains pretty well hermetically sealed against any manner of persuasion, but that has been true of others who have subsequently found or re-found a faith in God. Most of them, of course, had held to religious convictions at some point in their lives, and in spite of Dawkins' fondly remembered acquaintance with a benign form of Anglicanism and an equally benign Chaplain in his schooldays (*op.cit.* pp. 31 – 2), that cannot be said in his case. Yet we have seen how his arguments resonate with those who rejected religion in the 19th Century and there is no *prima facie* reason why the factors which drew many of them back to Faith should not prove equally compelling today.

In his stimulating account of how the Church lost its hold on the hearts and minds of English people, and how it might be recovered again, Stephen Platten quotes extensively from the poetry of Edwin Muir (Stephen Platten: *Rebuilding Jerusalem* SPCK 2007). Muir was raised on Orkney as a Presbyterian but relinquished his hold on faith as a young man. Or rather, in terms of the definitions we have been using, he relinquished his hold on religion. Platten comments: "In his poem 'The Incarnate One', he vents his frustration at the harsh and prosaic pattern of worship and living he imbibed as a child:

The Word made flesh here is made word again,
A Word made word in flourish and arrogant crook,
See there King Calvin and his iron pen,
And God three angry letters in a book ...
(Edwin Muir: *Collected Poems.* Faber 1960 p.228).

Later ... Muir came back to faith. But the faith to which he returned was more nuanced, more sacramental, and led Muir back into the mystery, the narrative, which lies at the centre of the Christian message" (Platten: *op.cit.* p. 174).

It is this "more nuanced faith" which we are advocating as the antidote to the kind of religion which repelled Muir and caused him and others to reject God. The nuancing lies in re-engagement with much that is precious in the realms of religion – word, worship, sacrament, symbol, celebration – but now with a clear sense that these are but the servants of a heartfelt trust in the reality, reliability and benevolence of One whose mystery relativises religion whilst ever continuing to inspire faith.

Christopher H. Partridge has written about "The Re-enchantment of the West" and has catalogued a wide range of indicators which point to stirrings of the Spirit where Secularism was believed to reign supreme (*The Re-enchantment of the West* T & T Clark 2005. See also: Jonathan Benthall: *Returning to Religion – Why a Secular Age is Haunted by Faith*. I. B. Tauris 2008). What is being described by Partridge as evidence of "re-enchantment" is pretty thin fare, as is much that passes for "spirituality" in modern culture. But one senses that if religion could itself re-engage with these stirrings so that a mess of New Age pottage might be flavoured and enriched so as to foster and feed this hunger for faith, then we may yet stand on the threshold of a new Crisis of Doubt – with Richard Dawkins leading the way?

Back to Modernity

"I have principles, and if you don't like them, I have others" (Groucho Marx).

One way of caricaturing religion is to portray it as essentially and irredeemably pre-modern. That is clearly where most of the European sceptics of the 18th and 19th Centuries were coming from, and as the 20th Century progressed the claims of the Age of Reason and the Age of Science gave rise to forms of positivism and empiricism which left little room for religious sentiment.

But this may not be quite so much of a caricature as is sometimes supposed. It is possible to interpret the response of organised religion to the likes of Galileo and Darwin as being symptomatic of a mindset implacably resistant to modernity in all its forms. Because religion formalises Faith, its very formalism militates against paradigm shifts in patterns of knowledge and what counts as evidence for truth. This will be exacerbated when a premium is placed on scriptural revelation and the traditions of the Church as primary sources of information about the world and its workings. Whilst some room may be found for truths based on Natural Theology, when hard choices have had to be made then it is Scripture and Tradition which invariably hold sway with religious authorities. To that extent, religion does have a built-in pre-modern bias which goes at least some way towards explaining the crisis of credibility which has characterised attitudes to religion in post-Enlightenment western culture. Furthermore, the rise of religious fundamentalism has only served to fuel this sense of religion as in opposition to the modern world, with a determination not only to dis-invent the Enlightenment but the Renaissance as well.

On the other hand, faith as we have defined it need have little to fear from modernity. Freed from the formalising tendencies of religion, yet still enriched and resourced by both Scripture and Tradition, the person of faith remains open to the insights of reason, experience and experimentation. Faith need not be on a collision course with the Enlightenment even if that sometimes seems to be how it is in relation to religion. So if the tension between modern and pre-modern worldviews is reflected in a similar tension between religion and faith, and if there is too much religion in the world and not enough faith, then surely it is simply a matter of re-affirming faith in modernity and all will be well.

However, Modernity has taken a mistress. Once wedded to the Enlightenment with its twin attractions of reason and experience as necessary foundations for building an ever-better home for the human family under the parenthood of God, modern culture has sought solace in the arms of another. Postmodernism is the preferred paramour bringing new excitement and a frisson of risk to the lives of those bored by scientific positivism and suspicious of enlightened philosophies which collude with ideological enslavement.

What will be the end of the affair? Will modernity eventually forsake its long-time spouse in order to move in with this new partner - to cohabit, of course, as marriage would entail a commitment which goes against the postmodern grain? Or will modern culture try for an "open" marriage by attempting to play both home and away - a strategy which must surely end in tears? Perhaps the time will come, indeed may well have already arrived, when we come to our collective senses and see the superficiality of our dalliance with postmodernism so re-building our marriage by going back to Modernity.

Of course there are those who would modify the analogy and argue that postmodernism has simply spiced up our marriage to Modernity. It is a form of Late Modernism which has brought late-flowering love to a long-standing relationship. Because we are all modernists now, postmodernism simply serves to describe what it feels like to be modern. It is an account of the emotional landscape which Modernity has created. The Enlightenment challenged the authority of revealed religion on rationalist grounds and so opened the way for a subjectivist and relativistic attitude to Truth in the realms of faith and morals. This freedom from metaphysical constraints is now flourishing as postmodernism or, to be more exact, post-modernism.

This won't do. When we come to assess the main ways in which postmodernism has impacted on religion and philosophy we have to conclude that the break with any kind of foundationalism - be it revealed, rational or experiential - is a clear break with modernism. There are real dangers in trying to baptize postmodernism as a new and welcome recruit to the realms of religious consciousness. The attempt to abolish or to supersede critical, self-conscious reason, "would leave us resourceless to know the difference between fantasy and actuality, to discern the distortion between ideas and their realisation" (Gillian Rose: *Love's Work*. 1995 p. 118). This is the assault made on reason by postmodernism and to that extent it is different in kind, and not merely, in degree, from the essence of modernism. It is a new love, and not an old love flowering late.

Modernism must not underestimate the risks involved when consorting with postmodernism. Not only do we find the foundational footings of reason and experience crumbling beneath us, but we also fuel the gloatings of those who will rejoice to see modernism consumed by the bonfire of postmodernist vanities. As contemporary culture tires of its flirtation with postmodernism it finds itself in search of foundations once again. Pre-modern fundamentalism is certainly there to set out its stall replete with dogmatic truths and metaphysical certainty. The temptation to return to a preternatural innocence will be dangled before the bewildered victims of postmodernism's intellectual promiscuity, and there will be many takers. So it is vital for modernism to keep itself in good shape for when the marriage between Enlightenment values and contemporary culture needs to be consolidated and renewed.

At this point, we must take seriously the perceived weaknesses in the Enlightenment project. Surely the priority given to reason in the organisation of knowledge has sounded the death-knell for creative and aesthetic sensibilities. It has led to an intellectual elitism which privileges logic at the expense of imagination, deduction at the expense of speculation and tactics at the expense of vision. The accumulation of empirical data has become an end in itself with information replacing formation as the staple of education and training. The emotional, affective and self-expressive dimensions of the human person have been devalued in deference to "a concept of reason which appears to mirror a particular ideal of detached, male, rationality" (James Byrne: *Glory, Jest and Riddle - Religious thought in the Enlightenment.* SCM 1996 p. 229). By no means least, the Enlightenment project has failed to deliver on its high ideals of equality and toleration and its belief that human progress was to be achieved by the application of science and reason (see J. Reader: *Beyond all Reason - the Limits of Post-Modern Theology.* Aureus 1997 p. 4).

Even though much of this criticism is over-stated, its force cannot be ignored. But any project which pits itself against the worst excesses of ignorance, superstition, prejudice and infantile dependence on patriarchal and feudal authorities will be sometimes defeated by the odds stacked against it. It has been said that both the optimist and the pessimist are fools - though one is a happy fool and the other an unhappy fool. So the only valid stance is not optimism or pessimism, but realism, and modernists have had to learn to be more realistic in their aims and projections, rejecting scientism as "a narrow, one-sided over-rating of the benefits of science to the exclusion of other human experiences" (Ursula King (Ed.): *Faith and Praxis in a Postmodern Age.* Cassell 1998 p. 5). But King goes on to list the gains of Modernity as "the significance of the historical method, the insights of social and cultural anthropology, the autonomy of civil society and culture, the importance of secularity, the freedom of the individual, racial and sexual equality" (*Loc. cit.*) These are the gains which King believes even postmodernists will acknowledge, and if we throw in the "brave attempt to focus on what unites, rather than divides us ... ... an emphasis on toleration and belief in the universality of human nature" (Byrne: *Loc. cit.*), together with the achievements of scientific endeavour and social democracy, then the acknowledged failures of Modernity might well be out-weighed by its positive and sustained contribution to human-flourishing and the common good. Much remains to be done if the worst social and environmental excesses of scientism are to be mitigated but we are clearly entitled to see Enlightenment principles as better suited to that end than the claims of pre-Enlightenment obscurantism or postmodern eclecticism.

The prevalence of postmodernism in the present climate poses a particular challenge to liberal theology. Some of our contemporaries have become so besotted with Modernity's new mistress that they are prepared to let her dictate to them how and what to think. So John Gladwin's engaging account of how the postmodern tail might be wagging the theological dog remains relevant (J. Gladwin: *Love and Liberty - Faith and Unity in a Postmodern Age* (DLT 1998). However, there is absolutely no need for liberalism to capitulate to postmodernism. Even though, in the best traditions of liberal theology, we will want to take full account of prevailing cultural assumptions and hear the word of God speaking to us through the spirit of the age, still modernism has its roots in the protestant ethos of the late middle ages, and remains protestant in its stance over against the shallow inconsequentialism of postmodern culture. Operating in such a mode, liberalism has three tasks to perform:

The Prophetic task: Back to Modernity

In recent history liberal theology can be described as interpretative rather than prophetic. It has accepted the modern world as given, and has applied itself to making the good news of God in Christ intelligible and convincing to modern ears. With the tide of postmodernism at the full, it is now necessary to argue for Modernity as a coherent account of reality and a sound basis for constructing a contemporary theology. Postmodernism with its crises of identity and chronically suspicious mind; with its injunctions to "go with the flow" and to "pick and mix"; with its contention that "it doesn't matter what you believe, so long as you believe that it doesn't matter"; and with its ultimately self-defeating belief that no beliefs are ultimately reliable, must be exposed as the cul-de-sac it really is. We are reminded of Dostoevsky's *cri de coeur*: "God, if everything is permitted, then where's the fun in anything?" (Quoted in Richard Holloway: *Looking in the Distance*. Canongate. Edinburgh 2004 p. 97). But the challenge to postmodernism must be the prophetic challenge of a confident and robust liberalism which affirms the narrative of Modernity, rather than the challenge posed by a regressive form of Christianity which seeks to dis-invent the Enlightenment and so try to defeat postmodernism with a heady mixture of irrational dogmas and charismatic hysteria. The crisis of postmodernism may yet issue in a straight contest between a new Dark Age and a renewed Age of Enlightenment. Surely that prospect must summon modern believers to a robust defence of Modernity.

This prophetic task is made all the more urgent by the fact that so-called "liquid modernity" (see Zygmunt Baumann: *Liquid Modernity* (Polity 2000) has led to a degree of nomadic rootlessness which postmodernism purports to celebrate, but which in fact causes societies to become chronically dis-eased and dysfunctional. Appeals to pre-modern nostrums will find ready takers in such a climate so that all manner of irrationalities and superstitions are peddled at a price. On the other hand, postmodernism offers nowhere for the over-vaunted vagabond to lay either head or heart. So modernism continues to offer the most appropriate antidote to postmodern displacement, and a theology resourced by that reality is required now as much as ever before.

Also, there is a tendency to attribute to modernity all the evils which overtook the last century and which threaten us in this one – from gas chambers and gulags to climate catastrophe and nuclear annihilation. It is pretty certain that modern science possesses the capacity to counter such threats so long as there is the will, commitment and imagination to meet the challenge. But bad-mouthing modernity is not going to help us if it is modernity itself which has the means to make the difference. Pre-modern methods will not enable us to feed the world, save the planet and make poverty history. Neither will postmodernism which is all pretention and no substance: all froth and no beer. Only when we get back to modernity, with base-camp principles applied with a pioneering spirit of enquiry, enterprise and expertise will progress be made towards a secure and sustainable future. Of course these base-camp principles pre-date modernity – they are the classical values and virtues which the western world has inculturated through Christianity. But they must be re-appropriated in such a way as to redeem the realms of science and technology rather than make them scapegoats for human failure in the face of unprecedented opportunities. It is significant that Jonathan Glover's chilling account of "a moral history of the 20th Century" is entitled *Humanity* (Jonathan Cape 1999). Once again we are reminded that the heart of the problem is the problem of the human heart. Glover tellingly observes that "If Stalinism shows what can go wrong when Enlightenment ideas are applied wrongly, Nazism shows what can happen when unenlightened ideas are applied rightly" (p. 394). Only a theology which enables both heart and mind to engage positively with the modern world can enable Enlightenment ideas to be applied rightly – and as only the right application of Enlightenment ideas can secure our future, a theology predicated on "back to modernity" is as imperative as it is prophetic.

The Apologetic Task: Faith and Modernity

The prophetic task goes hand in hand with the task of Christian apologetics which has always been at the top of the liberal agenda. Sometimes this has taken the form of arguing for and defending beliefs which are consistent with Modernity (see, amongst recent examples, Paul Badham *The Contemporary Challenge of Modernist Theology* 1998 and Keith Ward: *God, Faith and the New Millennium* 1998), whilst others argue for a liberal tendency in theological method characterised by such marks as openness, honesty, provisionality, mystery etc. (see J. Saxbee: *Liberal Evangelism* SPCK 1994 and Peter C. Hodgson: *Liberal Theology*. Fortress 2007). The danger in the former approach is that it can result in what Steven Shakespeare calls a "new conservatism". The latter approach has the merit of equipping and empowering people of faith with tools of interpretation and discernment which can guide them through the landscapes of Modernity without foreclosing on God's truth.

The Evangelistic Task: Modernity and Faith

Modernity rejects the non-foundationalism of the postmodern cult. Postmodernism allows for the possibility of believing; modern believing affirms the importance of beliefs. The metanarrative of God in Christ, interpreted by reason and experience, is the gospel we proclaim. It is more of a tendency than a set of tenets; more tentative than a text. Yet it rehearses the tunes of tradition even as it relishes the melodies of modernity. Liberals and post-evangelicals can co-operate in sharing this good news because neither is required to collude with postmodern relativism. So there is hope that sterile conflicts between liberals and conservatives can be put behind us as we respond to the challenge of postmodernism with a shared acknowledgement that Modernity is integral to the gospel of the Christ-like God we seek to share with a Christ-hungry world.

Meanwhile, if liberals renew their commitment to these three tasks then they will remain faithful in their marriage to Modernity and so be of service to the postmodern victims of a broken home.

Evangelism Re-Visited

"Go and tell, but not until you've been and listened".

The publication of a book is probably the nearest a man gets to giving birth. The gestation period is conspicuous but still personal and private. Then suddenly something internalised enters the public domain in the hope of a welcome, but with the real risk of abuse and misunderstanding. My only published offspring is *Liberal Evangelism* (SPCK 1994). It was written to try and establish a bridgehead between liberalism which is characterised as having no gospel to proclaim, and evangelism which is characterised as intransigent and triumphalist. The result has been a series of responses which have served to underline the hurt caused by these caricatures and the release which comes from realising that liberalism has a certain content and evangelism a content which is far from certain. It is this realisation which enables the two to do business together, so that liberal evangelism moves from being a contradiction in terms and becomes a positive and productive partnership in mission. Let me explain.

Since the dawn of the Christian age, and especially since the dawn of the Age of Enlightenment, there have been those who have attempted to see Christianity and culture as mutually enriching and not mutually exclusive. This has generally elicited a knee-jerk response from those seeking to protect the purity of the faith in order to keep it uncontaminated by the prevailing social and philosophical environment. Attempts to interpret the gospel in contemporary terms or to re-negotiate received traditions in the light of new knowledge attract charges of reductionism, betrayal and idolatry. In terms of the relationship between faith and reason or Christianity and culture carts are deemed put before horses and the secular tail to be wagging the sacred dog. Indeed, the need to punish this aberration with appropriate severity has led the "traditionalists" to accuse "liberals" of evacuating the gospel of essential content in the interests of collusion with the prevailing world view. So liberal Christians were charged with having nothing to declare and nothing to contribute to a decade of declaration. This is clearly not the case, but there is a note of caution to be struck when it comes to the content of evangelism.

Certainty in matters of faith is seductive. It can seriously damage the health of those who seek after it. It is also dangerous. It can be seriously destructive in the hands of those who claim to possess it. Books by reconstructed evangelicals testify to the damage done by the abuse of power by those who claim to know for certain and so tyrannise others with that knowledge. The jibe of one politician against another that "I wish I was as certain of anything as he is of everything" will find an echo in many minds, but it is not a worthy aspiration. A sense of assurance is much to be treasured in emotional terms, but intellectual certainty is incompatible with faith and cannot be claimed other than at the cost of God's glory and as a sop to human pride. Yet we are experiencing something of a helter-skelter retreat into certainty as conservative Christians seek to counter the metaphysical scepticism of modernism on the one hand and post-modern nonchalance in the quest for truth on the other. There is a tendency to reach for pre-modern prescriptions in an attempt to dis-invent the Enlightenment and so re-capture the moral, spiritual and philosophical high ground. But the Enlightenment cannot be dis-invented, and it is a principal tenet of liberal Christianity that core Christian values would be sacrificed in the attempt.

Historically, dogma has been a rod with which the strong can afflict the weak, the rich can oppress the poor and men can suppress women. Dogmaticism is the handmaid of certainty in things religious, and evangelism has much to fear from guilt by association with such a tool of tyranny.

Of course, none of this argues against the quest for truth and the urge to be on the side of truth in our pursuit of what is good and right and worthy of praise. But we will never cease to be a people on pilgrimage to places yet unknown and our faith will be, as Seamus Heaney put it,

"to believe that a further shore
Is reachable from here".

To believe that that shore is reachable is very far from belief that the shores of certainty with respect to the meaning of God, the universe and everything have been attained and secured beyond question. A major contribution to the cause of Christian evangelism can be made by the liberal tendency in its openness, honesty, responsiveness and commitment to plurality.

These principles still stand, and I believe they remain valid. But in *Liberal Evangelism* they were supported by three metaphors which need to be re-visited in the light of the tension between religion and faith which has become more pronounced since the early 1990s and which has been central to our theme and variations.

Lifts and Stairs

In a large department store, you can choose whether to use the stairs or take the lift when making your way from floor to floor. Climbing the stairs will demand effort, and it will involve you being exposed to both the temptations and the delights of each successive department. Taking the lift is easier; as you occupy your secure little room, you move through the various floors safe from direct involvement with any department with which you do not care to do business. The user of the lift, like many religious conservatives, inhabits a secure and unchanging environment, while on the stairs we see the theological liberals struggling to come to terms with each new department and having to decide how to spend what he or she has available and how to choose wisely from what is on offer. As we near the end of the 20th Century, more and more people are being encouraged to take the safe and secure "lift" of Christian conservatism – with the operators not so much telling the lift occupant what is available floor by floor, as telling the floor staff what is available in the lift! Thus Christianity passes uncontaminated through the core of successive cultures like the air-conditioned lift through the shaft of a departmental store. But what if the stairs provide the only means whereby Christianity can truly develop its identity by engaging creatively – and therefore, evangelistically – with a variety of historical, geographical and social institutions? It may be laborious, risky, full of potential distractions – but if Jesus ever took the lift, it was from the mountain top after His resurrection; before that, it was all done the hard way! (*Liberal Evangelism* p. 1).

This is a fairly typical *fin de siecle* conceit which might tickle the fancy, but has it stood the test of time? Sadly, the answer is yes, and if anything it now seems altogether too timid and understated. Whether or not we sign up to Samuel Huntington's *The Clash of Civilizations* (New York 1996) thesis, and it does seem to have been effectively challenged by Timothy Gorringe, amongst others (T. J. Gorringe: *Furthering Humanity*. Ashgate 2004), still we cannot ignore the increased stridency which characterises religious discourse and debate in the current climate of fear and suspicion. Malise Ruthven has offered a convincing account of fundamentalist religion in its historical development, but with a particular eye to post-9/11 concerns (Malise Ruthven: *Fundamentalism: The Search for Meaning* OUP 2004). Meanwhile, commentators have been queuing up to provide more or less apocalyptic accounts of the rise of the American Right and the role of religion in current socio-political rhetoric (see particularly Chris Hedges: *American Fascists*. Jonathan Cape 2007 and Jacob Weisberg: *The Bush Tragedy*.

Bloomsbury 2008 pp 73 – 107). By no means least, the tensions now threatening to destabilize the Anglican Communion pit conservatives and liberals against one another with little time or patience found for dialogue and mutual understanding. Demands for an Anglican Covenant owe more to the formalising dynamics of religion than the imperatives of faith and trust which should be characteristic of communion within the Body of Christ. It is also noticeable that ecumenism within and between the mainstream religions is proving more difficult as they increasingly employ aggression as a means of defence, assert their self sufficiency and find it ever more difficult to enter into relationships of trust and mutual respect.

It will be more and more important in the current climate to apply to evangelism the marks of openness, honesty and humility which were celebrated by John Habgood in his *Confessions of a Conservative Liberal* (SPCK 1988) and further expounded in *Liberal Evangelism* (pp. 17 – 25). But the key word which now comes into play, and which features at the heart of our definition of faith, is the word trust. Whether we are in the conservative elevator or on the liberal escalator we must learn to trust one another. This will mean recognising and respecting each other's faith, and within that mutuality we can then share and compare, listen and learn, challenge and be challenged by each other's religions in ways that are so much more difficult when it is religion rather than faith which dominates our theological horizon and prevailing worldview. The gospel of trust must be an evangelistic priority as we draw on the example of Jesus and so encourage our sisters and brothers to entrust themselves to the reality, reliability and benevolence of Almighty God lest yet more towers, containing both lifts and stairs, come tumbling down.

Two Tunes

The second metaphor takes us to rural New England: Charlie Ives could hear two tunes at once. He inherited this ability from his father George who, as the band-master in the small town of Danbury, Connecticut, would arrange for his own band and another one to march past each other in Main Street while each played a different piece. It seems that the local population were not sympathetic to George's experiments, which they heard simply as a discordant cacophony. However, his young son heard something that greatly influenced his own creativity as he developed into one of America's greatest composers. Charles Ives is now honoured for his innovative music, which pre-empted European atonal music by several decades, and among his most celebrated compositions are those that recapture experiences in the Danbury of his childhood by the weaving together of simultaneous melodies, harmonies and rhythms. People at the time thought he "had his ears on wrong", and it was not until some years after his death in 1954 that an audience began to emerge for these daring, sometimes bewildering, but always compelling, compositions.

During the 19th Century it became increasingly necessary for Christian believers to come to terms with hearing two tunes at once. While one band marched up the street to the traditional strains of revealed religion, from the opposite direction came a band of miscellaneous moderns improvising for all they were worth on the instruments of science and reason. So long as they were at some distance from each other, it was possible to contemplate the scenario with amused detachment, but a state of confusion was bound to prevail at the point of meeting. Some tried to hang on to one tune and shut out the other, others tried to harmonize the two, while yet others simply covered their ears until peace had been restored! There were those, though, who became excited by the ways in which this encounter opened up new possibilities for sensing and making sense of God, the world and human experience. Like Charles Ives, they tried to hear both tunes at once and could thereby enter a world of sense and meaning that transcended what either could achieve on its own. It is this tendency to want to hear two tunes at once that characterises liberal Christianity as it seeks to live creatively with the truth-claims of both traditional orthodoxy and post-Enlightenment modernism. It is the attempt to listen to Christendom and contemporary culture simultaneously and to hear, even through the apparent discords, the truths of eternity in tune with today. (*Liberal Evangelism* pp. 15 – 16).

There is still a great deal of mileage in this metaphor, but as postmodernism is inevitably consumed by its own vacuity, we have to wonder whether the metaphor is itself too post-modern. There is clearly much to be said for hearing together the tunes of tradition with the melodies of modernity, and thereby hearing something which transcends what neither could convey alone. But maybe the point does come when we have to acknowledge that this is a luxury we can no longer afford. It is not possible to harmonise the two tunes either, so we can only turn up the volume on what we believe to be right lest we are drowned out by the mounting decibels of a competing and dangerous ideology. In fact, this is what is happening more and more as religious intransigence gathers momentum and threatens to sweep all before it.

But I want to modulate the metaphor rather than abandon it. We have seen how religion is rather too attached to pre-modernity and it dances rather too readily to the tunes of dogmatism, hierarchy, authoritarianism and institutionalism. However, we have also seen how, when religion is at the service of faith, it has an important role to play – its tunes still need to be heard beneath and in support of those which sing of a faith at ease with modernity and in debt, but not in thrall, to religion. It is a faith predicated on trust, and when it comes to evangelism we can only repeat how trust in God and one another is critical to the gospel we proclaim in a world at odds with itself and its Creator. All too often evangelism has been about enticing people into he embrace of religion when it must be about nothing other than a leap of faith into the arms of God. Trust must now be the tune which is heard above all others even as the marching bands of religion and faith pass by each other and go their separate ways.

Face Values

In the waters around New York is Ellis Island, where tens of thousands of European immigrants were processed prior to their admission to the United States or their return from whence they came. It is now a museum full of evocative echoes that remind us of a bitter-sweet episode in the growth of a great nation. Among the exhibits is a cartoon depicting twenty or so portraits of George Washington. Each is recognizably the same father of the nation, yet each is portrayed according to the characteristics or a particular immigrant nationality – Russian, Italian, Hungarian, Spanish, and so on. The cartoon illustrates how there is a George Washington for every new American, whatever their nationality or ethnic origin. Surely as much and more can be said for Jesus, whose many "faces" have already been depicted and celebrated by countless works of art throughout the ages and around the world. Indeed, a satisfying theological "party game" is to display a range of reproductions portraying different faces of Christ around a room and invite participants to match each face with one of a choice of captions – teacher, healer, Son of Man, Son of God, judge, friend, shepherd, King etc. The effect of this exercise is to bring home not only the reality of the fact that we have four distinctive portraits of Jesus in the respective Gospels, but that within each of those Gospels other faces are to be found comforting, challenging, disturbing and befriending us according to need and circumstance. Paul Tillich observed that "there can be only one Christ, but he must be the Christ for everyone" and it is in the various faces Christ shows to the world that each person in every culture can find Christ for themselves. (*Liberal Evangelism* p. 51).

Jesus continues to have many faces, and there is a face of Jesus for everyone – just as there was a face of George Washington for all those who came to find a new life in the New World. That remains vital to the gospel we proclaim as liberal Christians or, rather, it is vital to the gospel we proclaim whatever label we choose for ourselves (see Steven Shakespeare and Hugh Rayment-Pickard: *The Inclusive God* . Canterbury Press 2007). But in the years since that metaphor impressed itself on my mind, I have come to realise that it has something else to say to us which is different but equally important. Those immigrants not only found in the face of George Washington a face which met them in their individual identities and circumstances, they also gave to Washington something of themselves thereby changing the face of America boatload by boatload and one by one.

Perhaps my original interpretation of this metaphor was too much influenced by a religious tendency to see evangelism as a one-way street – all give and no take. As things turned out, the immigrants gave at least as much to the fledgling nation as they took from it and the American Dream has always been predicated on this reciprocity. Religion is rarely reciprocal in such a way. New adherents are expected to conform to what they find. On the other hand, faith has trust as its core commitment and trust understood in the light of God's faithfulness and Jesus' example is always reciprocal. Covenants founded on faith and trust issue in mutual commitments which are graceful and generous even when they are challenging and costly. Covenants which entail commitments, but where there is no trust, rely on mechanisms of regulation and enforcement to achieve their ends.

Evangelism inspired by a gospel of trust will offer a face of Christ to meet each individual where and as they are; evangelism inspired by a gospel of trust will also welcome the contribution each individual will make to fashioning the face of Christ, so that who they are and who He is will always be mutually enriching.

Liberals have a full gospel to proclaim and when we speak of the Christian gospel or the Christian message, it is in terms of a rich seam of inexhaustible riches, some yet to be discovered, rather than in terms of a defined and predetermined deposit of truths already revealed and ready-to-wear. On this reading, evangelism operates according to a dynamic of listening and responding in accordance with the dynamic of giving and receiving which lies at the heart of the mystery of salvation. This gospel will celebrate the richness and diversity of our traditions which, when handled with openness and honesty, offer points of contact with modern and post-modern people which can lead to life and life in all its fullness. Liberal Christianity is essentially Christocentric in its provenance and proclamation. The many faces of Christ provide many criteria with which to evaluate the myriad values and claims promoted in a pluralistic society. The many faces of Christ also provide many reasons to expect that such pluralism will be met by a Christ who is for everyone. The incarnational "big bang" has issued in an expanding universe of Christological truth that can never be exhausted, or exhaustively defined, so long as there are Christ-centred people ready to respond to a Christ-hungry world with the infinite resources of a Christ-like God.

After the frivolities of post-modernism, back to modernity is not a bad rallying cry – especially given the alternatives. Modernity has proved hostile to religion, but its spirit of inquiry and adventure makes it friendly to faith. Faith means trust, and when trust is in dangerously short supply the work of evangelism – bringing people to *faith* – acquires a renewed impetus and sense of urgency.

Conclusion

"Run the great race of faith and take hold of eternal life, for to this you were called, when you confessed your faith nobly before many witnesses" (I Timothy 6 vs. 12).

"The one thought that possesses me most at this time and, I may say, has always possessed me, is that we have been dosing our people with religion when what they wanted was the true and living God" (F D. Maurice 1844).

"Jesus came to save us from religion". (Paul Tillich)

Little seems to have changed since Maurice's *cri de coeur* so that now, as then, religion remains problematic. However, as we have seen, the issue cannot be simplistically reduced to religion bad, faith good. In one form or another, religion has typically been made the whipping-boy for a whole raft of ills perceived to have beset the world. Recent best-sellers by Richard Dawkins and Christopher Hitchens are but the latest examples of a genre which has given voice to a steady stream of scepticism through the centuries. Dawkins is somewhat exceptional insofar as he sees all people of faith as tarred with the religious brush and thereby guilty at least by association with the worst excesses of ignorance, intolerance and violent extremism. Most religious sceptics are rather more discerning and discriminatory when it comes to manifestations of faith and spirituality which they acknowledge to be probably harmless and possibly benign when it comes to enhancing moral and aesthetic sensibilities.

So Richard Holloway sees himself as having joined those for whom "religion is no longer a way of life that is possible for them", but who do not therefore "cease to be interested in spirituality or the inner life of the human community" (*Looking in the Distance: The Human Search for Meaning.* Canongate Books 2004). These are those who in relation to organised religion are creatively disaffiliated – they positively choose not to belong, but they continue to value those dimensions of faith and spiritual experience without which humanity would be sadly impoverished. They may not wish to use Maurice's language of "the true and living God" but they would want to associate themselves in some way with what he was advocating over against religion. When Christopher Partridge charts *The Re-Enchantment of the West.* T & T Clark 2004) this is essentially what he has in mind.

Yet I want to insist that attempts to rule religion out in order to rule faith and spirituality in are unwarranted and ultimately self-defeating. Religion has always had a vital role to play in guarding, nurturing and sustaining the life of faith and this continues to be the case. But it must only ever be a subservient role with all pretensions to secure its own primacy and self-importance thwarted before they can take root. So how can religion be most effectively at the service of faith?

Well, one approach is provided by Michele Benoit in *The Thirteenth Apostle* (Alma Books 2007 p. 348). This trivial but engaging novel revolves around a Monk called Nil who uncovers evidence of an Apostle who was numbered amongst Jesus' followers but who for various nefarious reasons has been written out of the script by the Catholic hierarchy. Whilst on the run, Nil lodges with a knowing old hermit who offers the following advice:

"You must never bear a grudge against the Catholic Church. She does what she has always done, that for which every Church is designed: to win power and then to keep it at all costs. ... The Church is a necessary evil, my son: its continual abuse of power must not lead you to forget that it is the repository of a treasure, the person of Jesus. And that without the Church you would never have known him".

This is a classic example of damning with faint praise, rather like the Jew in Boccacio's *Decameron* who returned from a visit to Rome and sought baptism on the grounds that any Church which could continue to stand despite the obvious degeneracy of its leaders must be of God! Yet the hermit, like the Jew, has a point. For all its faults, organised religion by formalising faith enables the treasures of the tradition to be protected and passed on through the generations. So as a particular expression of organised religion the Church is seen as "a necessary evil" for it is the Church which guards the Gospel of God in Christ, and for that it might expect to be forgiven many faults and failings.

The minimalist version of this role is that the Church "keeps the rumour of God alive". To have the option of putting one's faith in something or someone, rather than nothing or no-one, does require some kind of formal means whereby the object of one's faith and trust can be preserved for posterity. But when we describe religion as the formalising of faith, there is more to this than the functions of a curator or custodian of core texts, teachings and traditions. This is altogether too passive a purpose, and religion in the service of faith surely has a more active part to play .

At its best religion has an instrumental role in pointing beyond itself to the priority of trust as the defining dynamic of faith. We have defined faith as a disposition to trust, and such trust cannot itself be commodified, reified or mediated. It is characterised by Kierkegaard as "a leap of faith" and this can only be taken by that "solitary individual" who stands at the heart of his teaching. Yet this deeply personal and unmediated faith can be, or even must be undergirded by the treasure store of thoughtful wisdom, spiritual experience, theological reflection and well-tested traditions of worship and mutual enrichment which are the marks of true religion as the servant of faith. Just as the skydiver needs *pistis* to get on the plane and soar to 15,000 feet, so he or she needs *emunah* in order to make that leap into thin air. When the doctrines and disciplines, credal statements and codes of behaviour, corporate membership rules and rites of initiation, cultic practices and personnel, structures of organisation and authority, sacred scriptures and symbols which we associate with religion are directed towards the leap of faith which each one must make for themselves, then religion serves its crucial and only legitimate purpose. As John the Baptist pointed beyond himself to Jesus as the one for whom the world was waiting, so religion must point beyond itself to the priority of faith as a disposition to trust in the reality, reliability and benevolence of the living God. Somehow I think F. D. Maurice would not have minded people being dosed with religion if he believed the tincture would be conducive to the fostering of faith. Sadly, he was all too familiar with less positive manifestations of religion and we have seen further evidence of such manifestations across a wide range of contexts and concerns.

Perhaps an analogy can help to clarify the issues at stake here. Let us reflect for a moment on the meaning and purpose of Art. After all, here is an aspect of our culture, life and corporate experience which seems to share many of the characteristics of religion. Indeed, Michael Austin has explored the case for Art as Religion and Religion as Art, and although he does not believe that one can be collapsed into the other, he does believe that there is a symbiotic relationship between them such as to suggest that theology would do well to learn lessons from modern art when it comes to relating Christianity to contemporary culture (*Explorations in Art, Theology and Imagination*. Equinox 2005).

Austin quotes the sculptor F. E. McWilliam who warned that "if you take the mystery out of art you're left with nothing but design and illustration", and then he offers the following summary of his own thesis:

"What this book has attempted to do has been no more than to allow artists to speak in their own ways to men and women of religious belief. It has noted the following truths about authentic artists: they produce work of moral beauty, they embody or incarnate truth, they enable us to see and to know, they are life-givers, they bring us to judgement, they sow seeds which germinate secretly within us, they bring us to the edge of a mystery which is as vast and as exciting for them as it is for the rest of us yet they seem to know the way to it and can lead us there. It is little wonder that not only have art and religion been confused but that for so many art has replaced conventional religion. The galley has become the place of pilgrimage". (Austin *op.cit.* p. 167).

The key point here is that whilst Art and Religion are not the same, they do both share a common purpose which is "to bring us to the edge of a mystery ... they seem to know the way to it and can lead us there". The job of the artist is to point beyond themselves to a mystery, and even to lead us to the edge of that mystery, but then we are left to make our own response which neither the artist nor anyone else can make for us. It seems to me that this is precisely what the dynamics of religion should really be about insofar as it must point beyond itself to the mystery of God, and even lead us to the edge of that mystery, but then leave us to either retreat or make the leap of faith and trust. This enables us to paraphrase McWilliam: if you take the mystery out of religion you're left with nothing but routine rituals and empty rhetoric.

Eric Newton has observed that:

"the phenomenon of [the Byzantine] style that, despite its flexibility, absorbs and dominates the personality of the artist, and turns him into a mere tool in the service of a cause bigger than himself, is surely the most impressive feature in the history of Christian art". (*The Christian Faith in Art*. Hodder & Stoughton 1966 p. 50).

However, on the contrary, it is not difficult to show how in the history of Art repeated attempts have been made to patronise and domesticate its fundamental purpose so as to use it to serve for more mundane and self-serving agendas. The scenes depicting the triumph of power of the classical gods of Greece and Rome on the ceilings of the Pitti Palace in Florence were clearly meant to testify to the no less impressive power and achievements of the Medici. Likewise, great artists have been commissioned to depict their patrons in styles and settings suggestive of a grandeur and gravitas which might not have been quite so evident if the artist has been given a free hand. Perhaps it is significant that this tendency has been no less prevalent in relation to religious art. The great Pantocrator mosaics of Cefalu and Montreale in Sicily are products of the Norman colonisation of the island and are intended to engender the same degree of awe and submission as was engendered by the massive Cathedrals of Durham, Lincoln and Notre Dame. The Wilton Diptych in London's National Gallery shows the Magi depicted as Kings Richard II, Edmund and Edward the Confessor. Eric Newton has observed that "In many of the great mural paintings in the Venetian Ducal Palace one has the curious impression that the Doge and the Deity meet on equal terms" (*The Christian Faith in Art*. Hodder & Stoughton 1966 p. 148). In Mark Mills' novel *The Savage Garden* one of the characters stokes an argument at a dinner party by suggesting that Renaissance art was more about using illusions and tricks to convey the skill of the artists than to fulfil "the higher, sacred purpose their works were intended to serve" (Harper 2007 p. 224). Even more damning is Suzi Gablik's take on Julian Schnabel's "Portrait of God" in which, she says, God "is just another image to manipulate ... it is difficult to believe in the prophetic consciousness of someone so frankly out to get what he wants – personal success in the New York art world, not metaphysical truths" (*Has Modernism Failed*. Thames & Hudson 1984 pages 90 and 97. Quoted in George Pattison *Art, Modernity and Faith,*. SCM 1998 p. 6).

Whenever Art, be it religious or secular, manifestly serves

purposes other than "to bring us to the edge of a mystery" and to offer insights into "metaphysical truths" it betrays the highest ideals and the essential humility of its greatest exponents. They knew that Art must point beyond itself or else collapse beneath the weight of its own hubris. Likewise, religion must point beyond itself, and lead us to the edge of mystery, lest it presume to master the faith it must only seek to serve.

The importance of prioritizing faith over religion is clearly attributable to the damage religion can do when these priorities are reversed. Damage which is exacerbated when religion unconstrained by its subservience to a loftier purpose finds itself exploited by those who covet its power and influence, whilst finding faith in the living God uncongenial to their personal ambitions or ideologies – Brenkman's "entrepreneurs of the soul". But the plea for less religion in the world, and more faith, rests on something even more important. As we have defined it, faith entails a disposition to trust and it is arguable that erosion of trust is one of the most significant factors contributing to the fragmentation and destabilising of societies in the modern world. In the so-called developed world, successive opinion polls and research projects point to an increasing distrust of institutions, authority figures and established conventions of believing, belonging and behaving. This owes a great deal to the cultural *cul-de-sac* of postmodernism to which we have referred in an earlier chapter. But it also points to a very 21st Century "crisis of faith" in the sense that not only trust in God, but trust in one another has been eroded by an almost pathological fear of failure, rejection and isolation. In her very moving psychological novel *The Other Side of You* (Harper Perennial 2007, p. 147) Salley Vickers observes that "humankind seems pitifully ill-constructed for love. Confidence, *con fides*, with faith. It takes faith to love. But perhaps it takes greater faith to be loved".

Having the faith to love and be loved, to entrust oneself and one's interests to another in the knowledge that one is loved and trusted in return must surely go to the heart of what Jesus meant when He spoke of having life, and life in all its fullness (St. John chapter 10 vs. 10). To have such a reciprocal relationship of faith and trust with God enables just such a relationship of faith and trust with others, and the future health of our society, or even its ultimate survival, may depend on our ability to recover, nurture and sustain such faith and trust as this century unfolds. When religion seeks to resource such a recovery of faith and trust then it will contribute significantly to resolving the problems we face. But when religion sets itself up as the solution then it can only make the problem worse. This was how the situation was seen by those who featured in the 19th Century "crisis of faith" and who viewed the role of religion in relation to the socio-political conditions of that time "as part of the problem rather than the solution" (Sarah Budd: *Varieties of Unbelief: Atheists and Agnostics in English Society, 1950 – 1960.* Heinemann 1977, pp. 107 – 8). There is no reason to see things differently today.

What all this entails is that those who present and represent religion must readily acknowledge the provisional and penultimate status of its doctrines and dogmas, credal statements and codes of behaviour, membership requirements and organisational structures etc. etc. These can all in their various ways serve to challenge, change, support and sustain those still journeying towards the edge of mystery and the leap of faith, as well as those who are already people of faith requiring what only religion can provide as they seek to remain faithful and inspire faith in others. This is what is meant by religion being at the service of faith, and we must look further at what this will mean in practice.

Meanwhile, one of the positive by-products of postmodernism is that it actually encourages people to be suspicious of claims to absolute truth and ultimate authority. This can help to neutralise the more extreme attempts to promote fundamentalist and authoritarian religious regimes. But it can also have the effect of, on the one hand, discouraging those who believe faith and religion to be synonymous and so mutually suspect or, on the other hand, encouraging extremists to turn up the volume on the old time religion in order to drown out contrary voices. So we must beware of seeing current cultural scepticism about truth claims and authority status as being sympathetic to our argument here. By and large such scepticism is antithetical to any kind of foundationalism whereas we would wish to affirm foundationalism albeit authenticated by faith rather than religion.

Yet more needs to be said about the priority of faith and trust, because they are crucial to the cause of freedom. We nave noted Martyn Percy's studies of *Power in the Church* (Cassell 1998), and how definitions of religion in terms of power feature prominently in the literature of sociology and psychology. We know that trust cannot be coerced: it can only be freely given and graciously received. So the propensity of religion to seek, secure and exercise power, especially when it is being used to recruit God in support of alien agendas, further militates against religion having anything other than a subordinate role in relation to faith and ways in which faith is shown and shared. One way of understanding the name Jesus is in terms of freedom, with its root meaning as "to being into an open space". When Christian religion uses power to coerce assent to orthodoxy, obedience to authority and adherence to cultic norms and practices, then it denies the very name of the Lord it purports to proclaim. But when Christian religion is at the service of a liberal and liberating faith, then it is a service which is perfect freedom.

So what are the practical implications of distinguishing religion and faith and prioritising them in such a way? A number of implications have emerged in the preceding chapters. There are implications for the way we read the Bible and handle issues to do with Revelation and scriptural authority (chapters 3 and 6); for the way we receive traditional teaching including the doctrine of Redemption (chapter 2); for the way we read and learn from Church history from the first century through to the nineteenth and on into our own times (chapters 4, 9 and 10); for the way in which we apply theological principles to the expression of Christian faith and discipleship (chapters 1 and 5); for the way in which we fashion and resource the Church in this generation (chapters 4 and 8); for the way in which we relate as a Church pastorally, prophetically and evangelistically to the culture around us (chapters 7 and 11).

But there remain other topics which we do well to notice in the context of these reflections.

First of all, the way we worship is significantly affected by the way in which we view faith and religion. In his prospectus to help the Church regain its hold on the hearts and minds of the people of Britain, Stephen Platten describes how faith came naturally to residents on the Hebridean island of St. Kilda before the arrival of ordained ministers who established and enforced an austere religious regime (Platten *op.cit.* pp. 4 – 11). The way they had expressed their faith, not least in the way they worshipped, was characterised by joy and spontaneity. The rigours of Calvinist Presbyterianism soon put paid to that, and proved to be "one of the three or four key causes in the final collapse of the islanders' civilisation". This is a classic example of that formalising of faith which characterises religion and which can have devastating effects when it contrives to suppress rather than serve the natural instincts and rhythms of life which have already formed in faithful hearts and minds.

So it is little wonder that Platten places a premium on the provision of liturgies which resonate with the rhythms of daily life. He cites examples which have worked well in Wakefield Cathedral (*op.cit.* pp. 165-6), and this confirms our view that whereas the Church has traditionally offered Festivals in search of congregations, we now have congregations in search of Festivals. In recent times new patterns of worship have emerged to try and re-establish that hold on people's hearts and minds which Platten rightly identifies as emblematic of the Church of England in particular, and which is in danger of being lost unless steps are taken to "rebuild Jerusalem" here. Such steps must major on those natural instincts and rhythms of life which are conducive to faith, and the function of organised religion will not be to make people religious but to create environments where even the smallest spark of faith can be fanned into a flame. Worship is crucial because worship is the articulation of trust, and trust is at the heart of faith. Prayer is the most expressive way in which we entrust ourselves and our interests to the reality, reliability and benevolence of God – and praise is the most natural way to proclaim confidently i.e. *con-fides*, with faith, that we know ourselves to be loved and that love is reciprocated. When religion is prioritised, worship can so easily become no more than a ritualised routine. When faith is prioritised, worship can take wing as the mystery and majesty of God is celebrated in wonder, love and praise. Religion will continue to authorise its ministers, approve its liturgies and robe its choirs but now all and only for the sake of the God who is present, the people who aren't and the faith which beckons us to the edge of mystery, and beyond.

Secondly, we are embroiled in numerous deliberations and debates in the Church about inclusiveness issues and the extent to which religious organisations can be allowed to claim exemption from legislation designed to secure equality of opportunity for all people irrespective of race, religion, gender, sexuality or disability. Here the distinction between religion and faith can be illuminating because the promulgation and policing of rules excluding certain people and including others are far more likely to be about protecting religious scruples than fostering faith in God and mutual respect amongst faithful people.

For example, in the debate about women Bishops, it is likely that anxieties about "sacramental assurance" will surface early and often. The fear is that a communicant may not be able to be sure that, even though the Eucharistic President is a man, he has not got a woman somewhere in his ordination pedigree. If we really are people of faith who are disposed to entrust ourselves to the reality, reliability and benevolence of God in Christ, then it seems inconceivable that such trust would not be reciprocated by a heavenly father disposed to feed His children who draw near in faith. And note that the invitation is to draw near *with faith*. To be concerning ourselves at that moment with arcane questions about sacramental assurance is to betray our faith to the regimen of religion and that is greatly to be regretted.

Again, although I share the view that the overall tenor of scriptural references to homosexuality is negative, and this has been reflected in codes of morals and manuals of discipline throughout Church history, still I wonder whether religious rules and regulations based somewhat selectively upon scriptural texts can negate the grace of God which is equal to the needs of all just as all are in equal need of God's grace. Religion has its part to play in helping us to be aware of God's presence, open to God's word and obedient to God's will. But surely not at the expense of our faith in the over-arching and all embracing inclusiveness of God which is for all people, and not just for some people, and which ensures that God loves all of us as we are – and loves us too much to leave us this way. There is something rather squalid and unworthy about appealing to the rights of religious people to be exempt from good and generous legislation only so as to protect our purity from those who are perhaps least able to protect themselves. John Donne once thundered from the pulpit of St. Paul's Cathedral a warning for those who saw themselves as chosen ones and all "impure" believers as the chaff for the fire: "such uncharitable Judges of all other men, that will afford no salvation to any but themselves, are in the greatest danger to be left out ... Nothing hinders our salvation more than to deny salvation to all but ourselves" (*Sermons*, volume 6 no. 7 [13th June 1624] pp. 161, 163 and quoted by John Stubbs: *Donne – the Reformed Soul*. Penguin 2006 p. 397).

Perhaps those whose religious scruples demand the right to discriminate against women and homosexual people in the life of the Church would not go so far as to deny them salvation as well, but they do seem to be privileging the rigours of religion over against the liberality of God's love in Christ who is the author and finisher of faith (Hebrews chapter 12 vs. 2). If that is so then it reinforces our theme: there *is* too much religion in the world, and not enough faith.

Thirdly, we hedge ourselves about a great deal when it comes to who can authorise whom to do what in the life of the Church. This was touched on in chapter 9 where we reflected on the relationship between Ministers of Religion and People of Faith. So here I simply want to observe that we have become used to the idea that restrictions on who can baptise or administer last rites become somewhat otiose in situations of *extremis*. But we hold on fast to our restrictive practices in all other circumstances. Yet is it not the case that all of us are *in extremis* when we come as sinners before God in search of forgiveness or when as guests at God's Eucharistic feast we come knowing ourselves not worthy to gather up the crumbs from under His table? Perhaps many of our religious distinctions and demarcations are put into perspective when we realise that only our faith and trust in God's grace can heal us and save us in the extremity of our need. Religious scruple may require us to go and show ourselves to the Priest – but it is our faith which makes us whole (see Mark chapter 1 vs. 44).

Fourthly and finally, we cannot ignore the practical implications consequent upon the prioritisations of faith over religion when it comes to urgent matters of local and global concern at the turn of the 21st Century. If there has been a breakdown in trust between people in the developed world, elsewhere there is scepticism as to whether the richest nations can be trusted to deliver on their commitments to combat global warming, eradicate poverty and withdraw support from manifestly unjust and corrupt regimes. Whilst there is some justification for the view that the Judeo-Christian tradition has been responsible for the irresponsible plundering of the world's resources, it can also be argued that this is just another example of religion being recruited to undergird the political and economic interests of those with a stake in environmental exploitation. The fact of the matter is that wise and just stewardship of the creation entrusted to our care is a far more prevalent theme in the teachings of the great world faiths, yet it has not worked out that way. Only when religions break free from the vested interests which infiltrate and distort them will those who stand to suffer most and soonest from the effects of ecological disaster be disposed to see religion as part of the solution rather than the source of the problem. Likewise, those who need to act urgently and to do most in averting the crisis now looming over us must be disabused of their belief that religious teachings endorse the *status quo*, and helped to see how people of faith can be prophetic and practical partners in what is now a desperate race against time.

A similar story can be told when it comes to creating a culture of trust and co-operation to tackle poverty and the widening gap between rich and poor on a global scale. There is a "bias to the poor" in most mainstream religions, yet the propensity for religion to be hi-jacked by "prosperity" agendas putting self-enrichment before social justice, has made it difficult for them to be taken seriously as allies in the war on poverty. This notwithstanding the fact that people of faith have been to the fore in key campaigns to cancel crippling debt and make poverty a thing of the past. Similarly, it has been hard for the victims of injustice to see religion as on their side when religion is so often seen to have been recruited by those in power to justify their policies and programmes of oppression.

By no means least, the role of religion in many of the conflicts which ravaged the world in the 20th Century and on into our own times has been well documented. This is probably the area where the vulnerability of religion to appropriation by alien and ungodly ideologies is most apparent. Yet there are instances enough to suggest that faith has been the motivation behind many challenges to tyrannies of violence and oppression whether we look to eastern Europe in the late 20th Century or to Burma in the 21st. Those who routinely charge religion with tacit collusion, or even active co-operation with incitement to war and the suppression of freedom need to be honest enough to acknowledge the role played by people of faith in the cause of peace-making and peace-keeping – a role which requires the kind of courage and commitment which faith both engenders and sustains.

If religion is believed to be championing rather than challenging those who pollute, impoverish and oppress by their policies and practices the time has come to put religion in its place and re-affirm the priority of faith and trust in God, and in one another, as the gift we bring to the table where these challenges need to be faced and overcome. Religion is about the recruitment of God to serve our agendas – agendas which are all too often exploitative, unjust and impoverishing. Faith is about putting our agendas at the service of God whose will it is that all people should know such fullness of life as Jesus came to bring. This being so, there is clearly too much religion in the world, and not enough faith. Human power, for all its potential for good, in fact tends to be predicated on domination, exclusion and enforcement. God's power is predicated on love, inclusion, trust and freedom. Our vision for the 21st Century must be of faith freed from subservience to religion so as to promote such love, inclusion, trust and freedom for God's sake and for the sake of God's world and people.

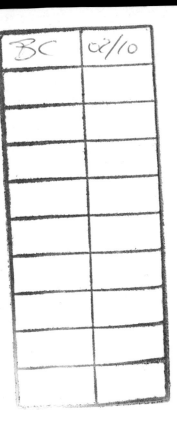

As one of the greatest of Christian theologians, Karl Barth wrestled more than most with issues to do with religion and faith. Adrian Hastings concludes that, according to Barth,

"all religions, at their best or worst, are mere human inventions, expressions of human pride, while the core of Christianity ... is something quite other, a divine revelation". (Adrian Hastings (Ed.): *The Oxford Companion to the Christian Church*. OUP 2000 p. 606).

Drawing on Kierkegaard's emphasis on the "infinite qualitative difference" between God and humanity, Barth eschewed any attempts to find a way from humanity to God, as we can only encounter God through God's own revelation and not at all through human reason or any kind of natural theology. This would clearly make him allergic to religion because, as we have seen, religion is too much about human agendas. Yet Barth has been at his most vulnerable when it comes to reconciling the human agency involved in the writing and interpretation of scripture with the need to preserve the autonomy of God and God's revelation. Inevitably his approach has led him to be seen as a chief advocate for the priority of faith and a form of fideism which continues to appeal to those anxious to resist the reductionist and humanistic tendencies of religion.

But his attraction to Kierkegaard's taste for paradox should have helped him to see that both *pistis* and *emunah*, Religiousness A and Religiousness B, religion and faith have a part to play in bringing the pilgrim on life's way to the brink of the abyss and then to make the leap of faith. Where Barth is crucial to 20th Century theology is in his trenchant challenge to religion as a vehicle whereby God can be recruited to promote causes far removed from God's word and will – something which Barth experienced at first hand in Germany during and between the two World Wars. What Hendrick Kraemer described as Barth's "merciless war-cry" against such tendencies (*The Christian Message in a Non-Christian World* (1938)) must continue to be heard because it reinforces our contention that there is, and probably always has been, too much religion in the world and not enough faith. However, the answer is not to argue, as Barth does, for the eradication of religion so as to clear the way for a radical affirmation of faith in God's revelation as the sole and sufficient path to salvation. Religion must have a role to play, but always a secondary role subservient to faith and the priority of faith in bringing all humanity within reach of God's gifts full of Grace and Truth.

***

As part of a ministry and mission review in a Devonshire market town, I interviewed a Police Sergeant in his sub-station strategically located in the pretty square. After opening pleasantries, I asked him about how the Church impacted on his work. "Hardly at all," he said, "sometimes I have to get the Vicar out of bed because lights have been left on, or I have to put out parking cones because of a big funeral. But otherwise I don't trouble them and they don't trouble me". As we talked further, I asked about what he thought was going well on his patch. It emerged that his pride and joy was the Victim Support Scheme which he had pioneered, and for which he had trained up 20 volunteers to visit and support those who had been on the wrong end of criminal behaviour. "Tell me," I said, "how many of those 20 volunteers are Church people?" He scratched his head for a moment, then said "Well I'll be damned, all of them!"

What had been for him a question about the Church as religion with its buildings, rites of passage and dog-collared personnel had turned into a conversation about the altruism, courage and witness of faithful Christians leavening the life of their little town. It was religion which motivated and resourced them, but it was faith which inspired and encouraged them. The Sergeant was not too sure he wanted too much of the former, but of the latter, he just couldn't get enough!

B O O K S

O is a symbol of the world, of oneness and unity. In different cultures it also means the "eye," symbolizing knowledge and insight. We aim to publish books that are accessible, constructive and that challenge accepted opinion, both that of academia and the "moral majority."

Our books are available in all good English language bookstores worldwide. If you don't see the book on the shelves ask the bookstore to order it for you, quoting the ISBN number and title. Alternatively you can order online (all major online retail sites carry our titles) or contact the distributor in the relevant country, listed on the copyright page.

See our website **www.o-books.net** for a full list of over 500 titles, growing by 100 a year.

And tune in to myspiritradio.com for our book review radio show, hosted by June-Elleni Laine, where you can listen to the authors discussing their books.

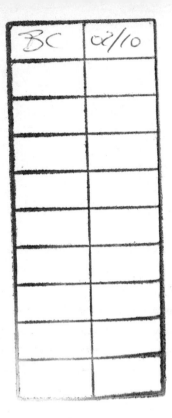

BC	02/10